becoming a
category of one

becoming a category of one

How Extraordinary Companies Transcend Commodity and Defy Comparison

Joe Calloway

WILEY

John Wiley & Sons, Inc.

Published by John Wiley & Sons, Inc., Hoboken, New Jersey.
Published simultaneously in Canada.

For general information on our other products and services please contact our Customer
Care Department within the United States at (800) 762-2974, outside the United States
at (317) 572-3993 or fax (317) 572-4002.

Wiley also publishes its books in a variety of electronic formats. Some content that
appears in print may not be available in electronic books. For more information about
Wiley products, visit our Web site at www.wiley.com.

Library of Congress Cataloging-in-Publication Data:

Calloway, Joe
  Becoming a category of one : how extraordinary companies transcend
commodity and defy comparison / Joe Calloway.
        p. cm.
  Includes bibliographical references and index.
  ISBN 0-471-27404-6
  1. Benchmarking (Management)   2. Corporate image.   3. Brand name
products.   I. Title.
  HD62.15.C34   2003
  658.4′013—dc21

                                                        2003002423

Printed in the United States of America.

10   9   8   7   6   5   4   3

For Jessica Rose Calloway
and answered prayers.

Contents

Preface   ix

1   We Just Decided to Go   1

2   Know Who You Are   24

3   Success Means You Know What
Used to Work   51

4   The Commodity Trap   74

5   Your Brand Is Everything   97

6   The Three Rules   122

7   The New Customer Reality   145

8   Case Study—Tractor Supply Company   168

9   The Heart of a Category of
One Performer   195

Index   217

About the Author   223

Preface

Don't strive to be a leader in your category. Create a different category, and be the only one in it. That's the idea behind *Becoming a Category of One*.

For over 20 years, I have had the privilege of working as a consultant and business speaker for some of the best companies in the world. In that time, I have become fascinated with those companies, large and small, that are able not only to achieve success, but sustain that success over time and in such a way that they truly stand out as a category of one.

There are lessons to be learned from these companies: lessons that can be immediately applied to your business, whether you are in a large corporation or are a one-man band. Some of the lessons might surprise you. If you're looking for rocket science, you won't find it here. The lessons are as simple as they are challenging. Perhaps the most surprising lesson of all is that quite ordinary people who simply do what other people are not willing to do achieve extraordinary success.

There are common threads that run through extraordinary companies, regardless of the size of the organization or the industry that they're in. Some of the companies we discuss you will be familiar with, most of them you will never have heard of. What's most amazing to me is that these Category of One companies are everywhere. You've got them in your neighborhood and you know people that work for them. They range from big retail operations like LensCrafters and Tractor Supply Company, to companies "flying under the radar" of the popular business press like an outrageously creative film production company or a small but remarkable dental practice.

Much of this book is about those Category of One companies that exist right under our noses. Companies not that different from yours and mine that have created something really special because of the way they do what they do. There are many books on the shelves about the "usual suspects." The Southwest Airlines success stories (and I relate one of those stories in this book) that we all know so well are inspiring, to be sure. But what I find more inspiring and often of more practical use are the stories of how a farm and rural supply store or insurance brokerage group or cell phone sales manager have managed to rise to the top level of performance and success.

What's truly remarkable is the commonality of the threads of extraordinary success that weave themselves through this diverse mix of companies. What works for the small, 10-person company is precisely the same as what works for the billion-dollar corporation. These ideas aren't mine. I'm just the reporter. Hopefully, I've learned a few things about business success along the way, but I'm not the expert here. The experts are the people that you'll find in this book who have taken their businesses to the next level of performance, and do so on a continuing basis.

Becoming a Category of One company begins with a conscious decision. Every company that I studied had the experience of a "moment of truth." For some, it was a "fish-or-cut-bait" experience, in which they decided either to take their business to that next level of performance or close the doors and do something else. Some companies found greatness because of a crisis, others because they recognized that they had become complacent with their level of success, and weren't willing to settle for that.

Each of these extraordinary companies also has a clear sense of who they are. They all define themselves, not in terms of what they sell, but in terms of *what the point is* for their employees, stakeholders, and customers. The drive to serve, accomplish, and achieve is much more powerful than the drive to simply make more money or sell more widgets. It's not that these companies are made up of save-the-world-do-gooders. All of the Category of One people I met and spoke with have a keen sense of competition, and every one was a savvy businessperson. But they all had a larger purpose that was tied to the significance of what they were doing.

The willingness to let go of what used to work is, for many of us, the most daunting challenge of all. Category of One companies not only let go of what got them there, they throw it out the door regularly to make room for what will work next. The trap of past success is a seductive, almost irresistible force. Category of One leaders constantly encourage their employees to look for the next great idea, even if it is met initially with derision and criticism. It takes real courage to innovate and real leadership to create the space for innovation to take place.

Your customers see you as a commodity, just as they see every other business out there. You will continue to be seen as a commodity, and be forced to compete on price, until you do something that transcends being a commodity in the customers' eyes. Only when you differentiate yourself in a clear and powerful way can you become a Category of One company. Even quality companies like BMW have learned that quality is no longer the differentiator it once was. You must create a compelling customer experience to win in today's marketplace.

Your brand is everything. By brand, I don't mean your name, your logo, or your advertising. That's not your brand. That's how you try and tell the story of your brand. Your brand is who you are, what you promise, and your ability and willingness to keep that promise. Every Category of One company is dedicated, throughout the organization, to building, communicating, and protecting the brand. Your brand resides in the minds of your customers and potential customers. It's who they think you are. It's about people keeping promises.

Across all industry and professional lines, great companies large and small are driven by a focus on one factor: the customer. The three rules that Category of One companies all follow are:

1. Know more about the customer than anyone else does.
2. Get closer to the customer than anyone else.
3. Emotionally connect with the customer better than anyone else.

To take care of the customer may seem like the oldest business philosophy in the world, and indeed it may be, but what I found amazing is how few companies actually base their businesses on that philosophy. Category of One companies, without exception, are dedicated to winning and keeping loyal customers for life.

Your customers' expectations are higher than they've ever been. And tomorrow they'll be even higher. Your customers compare you to everybody, not just the other companies that do what you do. Category of One companies look for ways to improve by benchmarking the entire marketplace, not just their own defined category of business. A bank might find its next best idea from what the hospital down the street is doing with customer relations. You have to look everywhere for your customers' new standards of performance.

For my Category of One case study, I chose what I consider to be one of the best companies in the world, Tractor Supply Company. If you haven't heard of them, you probably will someday soon. The people at Tractor Supply Company have taken the oldest, most basic business principles in the world and made them the foundation for a company that succeeds by any standard. The loyalty of their customers is legendary and the spirit of their employees is inspiring. The lessons on leadership that Joe Scarlett and Jim Wright can teach us through their beliefs, ideals, and everyday actions are among the most meaningful that I have ever experienced. It has been my great pleasure to watch Tractor Supply Company grow and prosper for 20 years. I thank them for their willingness to share their principles of success in this book.

Finally, I offer discussions with some very special people that I feel reveal the heart of a Category of One performer. From Dr. Cheryl Scott's dedication to constant learning to Jane Hutson's drive to help others succeed, the lessons offered in these candid and honest interviews can benefit anyone in any business that wants to take their own performance to the next level.

Writing this book has been a humbling and deeply satisfying experience. With all the negative news about business and corporate America that we've seen over recent years, I come away from this project with a renewed faith that doing the right thing works, treating employees and customers fairly and with respect will lead to success, and that the good guys really do win. My hope is that this book is helpful to you and your business in *Becoming a Category of One*.

We Just Decided to Go

It's Not a Miracle

The movie *Apollo 13* opens with a gathering of astronauts at the home of Jim and Marilyn Lovell to watch the live television broadcast of an incredible event. Their fellow astronaut, Neal Armstrong, is about to become the first human being to set foot on the moon. There is a light-hearted, party atmosphere among the group. But as newsman Walter Cronkite announces the event, and we hear Armstrong's immortal words, "One small step for man; one giant leap for mankind," the mood becomes quiet, almost reverential. Even Cronkite, the veteran newsman with years of covering historic world events, seems nearly overwhelmed with the enormity of the moment.

Shortly after the broadcast, the party breaks up and everyone goes their separate ways. Jim Lovell, who is played by Tom Hanks, is now alone with his wife Marilyn in their backyard. Looking up at the moon, Lovell says, "From now on, we live in a world where man has walked on the moon. It's not a miracle. We just decided to go."

Deciding to go is the first step on the journey to becoming a Category of One. Unfortunately, it's also the step usually not taken. Most companies never decide to go. They never make the decision to become extraordinary. The decision they make is to *talk* about becoming extraordinary or to *have meetings* about becoming extraordinary or to *write mission statements* about becoming extraordinary. But they never "decide to go," that is, make the commitment that takes hold, becomes real, and creates a new level of success.

A Deliberate Decision

One of the common threads I've observed among extraordinary companies is that they make very deliberate decisions to go in terms of pursuing greatness. The decision can take many forms. It might be a decision that is initially made by one person, maybe the president of the company. It could be a group decision reached over a period of years, culminating with someone in a meeting saying, "Let's do this thing. Let's see how far we can go, how much fun we can have, how much money we can make." But at some point, most extraordinary companies make a clearly defined decision to go. It literally comes down to a moment of truth. Then, to sustain their success, they must recommit to that decision again and again.

Turning Points

Category of One companies can almost always point to a very specific time when they made a decision to go. When asked if there was a turning point for their company, I've had company presidents tell me things like "In 1979, we were face to face with a real crisis. That's when everything changed and we started taking things in the right direction," or "It was at the annual company convention in 1995. One night some of us were talking at dinner about the future and what we hoped to achieve, and, all of a sudden, we just looked at each other and decided to do things differently."

Sometimes the seeds for the decision to pursue greatness are planted from the bottom up, rather than from the top down. Rather than the top people in an organization making the decision to go, their job might best be seen as creating a culture and an environment that is supportive of everyone in the organization seeing opportunities for growth and then acting on them. When a major decision to go comes from the top down, then it must be thoughtfully communicated within the organization and given the chance to gain the support of the employees. Almost every extraordinary company can point to a very specific moment in time when the decision was made to be great. The implementation of that decision is a continuing process, but the decision itself is a very clearly defined and identifiable event.

The Value of a Crisis

Very often, great companies become even greater when a crisis forces the decision to go. There's a tremendous sense of clarity and urgency that can come from facing disaster. It's in these moments of truth that the true Category of One company rises to the top. For extraordinary companies, a crisis can "thin the herd" and invite the competition to find another line of work.

Larry Keener, CEO of Palm Harbor Homes, one of the nation's largest producers of manufactured homes, says that they have had two critical moments of truth in the company's 24-year history. The first occurred in the late 1980s when the industry was experiencing a cyclical downturn. "Downturns are wonderful validators of core strategies," Keener says.

"What we learned during the 1980s moment of truth was twofold. First, that just hiring good people would not produce high quality homes, satisfied customers, and high associate retention. We needed a well-defined quality system supported with broad-based training consistent with our mission. The system we installed was a customized version of Philip Crosby's Quality Improvements Process (QIP). It has become our 'religion' and nearly a universal answer to any 'how' questions of performance improvement."

Palm Harbor also discovered, during the 1980s downturn, that their independent retailers, as a group, did not share the company's vision or commitment. As a result, their efforts were only as effective as their least effective retailer. To control their future and the integrity of their brand, they got into the retail business.

"These two decisions were outside the mainstream of our industry," Keener says. "They both required enormous investments and patience. However, today our ability to control our processes within defined quality tolerances and our ability to uniformly deliver to every customer the value and quality they want, is our greatest separator versus our competitors."

Forced to Expand Our Definition

The second decision to go for Palm Harbor Homes was prompted by a crisis caused by the good economic times of the

1990s. "That moment of truth concerned retail home financing," Keener says. "Our industry is cyclical and the cycles are driven by retail financing. During the good times of the 1990s, independent industry finance sources bought too deeply into the weaker credit customer pool. As a result, defaults have soared, lenders have failed, and others have retrenched. There was a dearth of outside lenders to our industry."

Palm Harbor's demand for its homes remained high throughout the cycle because of brand-building advertising and their ever-expanding customer referral pool of prospective new homeowners. Yet, their sales were constrained to the same degree as the rest of the industry from the lending excesses created by others.

"We knew that our commitment to become 'legendary' and to be 'an extraordinary company in an ordinary industry' was dependent on our ability to provide credit to creditworthy buyers," Keener says. "We have started a mortgage bank. It's the first in-house mortgage bank in the industry, and we will have a full-fledged consumer lending company soon. Our philosophy is that if a customer deserves credit, they deserve a Palm Harbor home; and, if they deserve credit, Palm Harbor should provide that credit to them."

Palm Harbor's moments of truth when they decided to go were spawned by industry crises. They were forced to expand their definition of themselves and their commitments. "We have had to evolve and expand our span of control to keep our commitment to our customers and ourselves," Keener says. "We have always wanted to be a great company. Circumstances keep redefining the requirements of 'great.' We view these circumstances as opportunities to separate ourselves from the competition."

Go Big or Go Home

Quill is a subsidiary of Staples, Inc., and is a leading direct marketer of office supplies. In the mid-1980s, the three original owners of Quill realized that the business had grown beyond them. They wanted Quill to sustain its history of growth, exceptional customer service, and operational excellence, and knew to do so would require taking the company to the next level of performance. A decision was made to bring in three experienced executives from outside the company. This was Quill's specific moment in time that changed everything about their future. From that point, the company was able to challenge its old ways and become more aggressive. They stopped doing initiatives and tasks only in a linear fashion.

The second moment of decision came when Staples, Inc. purchased Quill. A mandate came from the new corporate parent to grow the business faster. Larry Morse, president of Quill, describes the decision-making process. "Our whole senior management team met off-site for two days and decided that we needed to become a high-performance organization in every way possible," Morse says. "We committed ourselves to driving for excellence in everything we did, especially in the area of customer service, and that became our mantra. In fact, we came out of that meeting with a slogan that depicted our new approach to business, 'Go big or go home.'" This off-site meeting was Quill's second critical turning point.

In both cases, the decision to go was made by senior leadership teams. In the first case, the owners did a lot of soul searching together and decided that they were not going to hang up the "gone fishing" sign, but rather ignite their company to reach new levels of growth and success.

The senior leaders were imbued in the Quill culture and that group was anxious to put their mark on the company and drive for success. While the chief executive rallied this group, it was easy to get them to take the plunge.

Most companies never get beyond the talking stage of the decision to go. Even though they think they've committed to doing something different and significant, what they've really done is just commit to *talk* about doing something different and significant. Quill's commitments included much more than just talk. They developed five strategic imperatives that provided the framework for their planning:

1. Maximize our customer base.
2. Develop a contact and relationship model that enables Quill to sell and service more effectively.
3. Deliver and promote the best service and value in the industry.
4. Drive toward deeper product and market penetration.
5. Achieve operational excellence in everything we do.

Quill didn't just talk about taking the company to a new level of performance. They made the decision, then immediately began to implement changes in how they did virtually everything. That's the difference between companies that go, and those that don't. The decision to go is followed by immediate and significant action. There's a clear signal being sent within the company that there's something big going on here and it's made real by action. A vision without execution is just an hallucination.

A Dangerous Assumption

Some might say, "But it goes without saying that everyone in our company wants us to be the best! Of course we all want to be great." Well, it doesn't go without saying. And even if they are saying it, it doesn't necessarily mean that they believe it, or even that they want it. There are many companies that mistakenly assume that all employees not only want to be the best, but, more important, are willing to do what it takes in terms of commitment, change, and hard work to make it happen. This is often a false and sometimes a dangerous assumption.

There are many people out there, maybe even most of the people out there, who don't aspire to greatness. That's not necessarily a bad thing. There's absolutely nothing wrong with wanting to live your life simply doing a good job. Some people want to be in the parade. Some people want to lead the parade. And some people just want to watch the parade go by. Of course there are also people who live, as Thoreau said, "lives of quiet desperation." These people are in survival mode, quite possibly through no fault of their own. Achieving greatness is the furthest thing from their minds. They just want to make it through the day.

I'm a fairly high achiever, but I must admit that there have been times that I thought I would scream or even do bodily harm to someone if I heard one more motivational speaker talk about following my bliss or finding passion in my work. Sometimes I just didn't feel like scrambling up the ladder of success. I just wanted to claw my way to the middle and stay there for a while. But to reach my potential, I realized that I had to come to that "moment of clarity" decision. I had to decide to go.

Many of the same dynamics apply whether you're talking about achieving the very personal aspirations of an individual or the goals of a multinational corporation. In either case, nothing of substance will take place without commitment. On a personal level, I'm embarrassed to admit that I was a cigarette smoker for many years. Although I knew that I had the will power and ability to quit smoking, the fact was that I didn't really want to. I would set a goal of stopping smoking and stick with it for a few weeks, but ultimately end up right back where I started at about a pack of cigarettes a day. The one reason I continued to fail was that I had made the intellectual decision to stop smoking, but not the "gut" decision.

Companies do the same thing. I once did some consulting work with a bank that claimed it wanted to increase sales in its national accounts division. What they did was double the number of calls that each sales representative was required to make each week, thinking that this would double the sales. The very predictable result of this ridiculous strategy was that as the quantity of calls increased, the quality of each call suffered tremendously, and sales actually fell.

I advised the bank to work on reducing the number of calls they were making, but put more time into the research and preparation for each call, thus dramatically increasing the closing ratio. But this would have required more change and more work than they were willing to undertake. So ultimately they got what they really wanted the most, which was just more activity and the appearance of improvement.

We Get What We Want the Most

You may be wondering what I mean by saying they got what they wanted the most, when what they "said" they wanted was increased sales. Talk is cheap. Actions speak louder than words. I'm rolling out the clichés because they are true in this case. It's like someone saying that they want to lose weight then ordering the triple cheeseburger with bacon instead of the salad. What they wanted more than to lose weight was to eat the cheeseburger. It's not rocket science here. We get what we want the most.

Take the bank I was just talking about. They said they wanted increased sales but they weren't willing to do the research and planning necessary to make that happen. It was just too hard and they weren't willing to go there. What they really wanted the most was to talk about increasing sales but in reality increasing activity was the easy way out. It would give the appearance of striving for success without having to do all that heavy lifting involved in preparation and research.

I've seen a thousand versions of the same story over the years from all kinds of companies. They say, "We want to have the best people in the world" but they won't invest in training or better hiring practices. They say, "We want our people to take responsibility" but they don't give them any real decision-making authority and they second-guess everything their people do. They say, "We want teamwork" but they do nothing to improve communication between departments. What they really want is the status quo with slogans. Or they want different results while doing exactly the same things they've always done, which some say is the definition of insanity. They should summon up the courage to just admit that they want to talk a good game instead of playing one.

We Don't Want to Go

There's a wonderful scene in the movie *Butch Cassidy and the Sundance Kid* where Butch and Sundance are sitting on the balcony of the local house of ill repute, watching the sheriff in the street below. The sheriff, who thinks that the outlaws are on the run and far away, is trying valiantly, with all of the inspirational, motivational, and oratorical skills at his command, to raise a posse to track down Butch and Sundance and bring them to justice.

As he implores the group of townspeople to join him in this quest for justice, his audience just stares at him, obviously not moved one bit to saddle up and put themselves in harm's way. They just listen and stare. They might be cowardly, but at least they are painfully honest in their lack of commitment.

Nobody's playing any games or displaying any false bravado. They don't want to go. And they're not pretending that they do. What this means to the sheriff, the would-be leader of this posse that just won't become a reality, is that at least he knows where he stands. Better to find out in town than out on the range when they're far from home. Don't saddle up and charge ahead if you're just kidding around.

Let's Have a Pep Rally!

We are a society that loves parades, pep rallies, and celebrations. The same holds true in business. We love to set lofty goals and celebrate what we hope will become reality, but we've not been willing to make the required commitment to change.

Everybody talks a good game. Every company gives lip service to taking performance up a notch and being the best that they can be. We pick a theme for the next company meeting: Riding the Waves of Change! . . . Dominate the Market! . . . Total Customer Satisfaction! . . . The Success Zone! . . . The Power of One! . . . The Power of the Team! . . . The Power of

Partners! . . . (how about The Power of Slogans!) . . . Achieving Excellence! . . . Breaking Down Barriers! . . . Thinking Outside the Box! . . . Setting the Sails for Success! . . . Creating Excellence! . . . or, that perennial favorite, Exceeding Our Customers' Expectations!

In planning that next big meeting, we do everything we think we're supposed to do. We fly everyone to a great hotel in Cancun or Hilton Head or some other appropriately sunny beach location. The company executives make rousing speeches about vision and mission and celebrating our successes while looking ahead to further heights of greatness. The experiential training consultants facilitate team-building exercises on the beach, which consist of breaking into teams and figuring out ways to make a functional raft out of the odd assortment of materials we've been given to work with. We have breakout sessions on new products and systems. After every meal, there's a motivational speaker who gives us an inspirational message about being your best no matter what the odds are against you, and the importance of throwing that one starfish back into the ocean. There's the awards dinner and dance with the oldies band and, quite possibly, the mass hysterical group dance performance of "YMCA." How could it be any better?

Then, on the last day, there's the closing general session. The big finish. The session that will send us back into the world riding a motivational tidal wave of epic proportions. The president of the company gives a speech that invariably begins with "Well, we've had an incredible three days here, but there's much more to do." The final mountain-climbing, obstacle-overcoming motivational speaker gives a barn-burner of a chest-thumping speech and whips the room into a frenzy of thunderous and wildly cheering employees as the sound system blares Tina Turner singing "Simply the Best" at warp volume, while photos of smiling, thumbs-up employees in various poses at their work stations and in their cubicles are projected onto the giant screens on either side of the stage. The motivation is palpable. It's in the very air that we breathe. We foam and froth, and the room comes dangerously close to spontaneous combustion. We join hands and sway in giddy unison to the sounds of Queen's "We Are the Champions." And then we go home.

Back at the office we cover our walls with attitude boosting posters featuring glorious color photographs of eagles soaring above the clouds, snow-topped mountain summits, and teams (in which there are no I's) crossing the finish line in sweat drenched celebrations of victory and dreams come true. In our homes, we tape personal success affirmations to the bathroom mirror and read them every morning before we listen to the motivational tapes in the car on the way to work. Surely we are doing everything necessary to scale the summits of success.

What Happened?

Six months later, people stare into their affirmation covered bathroom mirrors and companies look at their less than hoped for numbers and they wonder what went wrong. The goal of truly taking performance to a new level wasn't reached. The eagle didn't soar to the mountaintop. Maybe your competition turned out to be simply the best and you're still second. And what's often most deeply frustrating in these situations is that the failure to achieve these goals happens to companies who seemingly have everything going for them, including great people, sound business strategies, and excellent products.

So what happened? With all the best-laid plans and all the spine-tingling motivational cheerleading, they never took the critically important first step. They never *decided to go*. Not really. They just talked about going.

Answer the Tough Questions

But wait! Surely they decided to go! Why else would they have taken the time and trouble to put up the posters and play the music and have the meetings and tape all those affirmations to their bathroom mirrors? Because they were willing to do the easy stuff. The hard stuff is reaching deep down inside and looking honestly into your soul and asking, "Do we really want to do this and are we willing to change how we've done it up to now?"

I give many speeches about building brands and competitive strategies, which means that I go to a lot of corporate conventions and meetings. Believe me, you can't predict the probable success of a company based on the look or sound of its meetings. Quite often, it's the quietly determined companies who don't make much noise that are the ones who actually walk the talk. Enthusiasm isn't necessarily loud.

That's not to say that big budget meetings can't help produce big results. They can. Sometimes what's needed to create momentum and enthusiasm is a good dose of fun, show business, and motivation. It's not that there's anything wrong with the big company meeting at the big resort hotel. It's just that for it to produce something worthwhile, it must be accompanied by the commitment to make something happen.

In my presentations, I confront companies with some simple yet very tough questions about their stated goals: "Do you really mean this?" "How far are you willing to take this thing?" "What's your tolerance for chaos?" "How scared are you able to be and still function?" "Are you willing to let go of everything that works in order to get to where you say you want to go?" "Who are you?"

"What do you really stand for?" "When it comes right down to it, what's really important around here?" "When you say that your intention is to be the best in the business or to achieve true excellence or to take your business to the next level, are you serious or are you really just kidding around?"

There are very serious ramifications involved if the answer is "Yes, we're serious." The reality may be that you and your company just may not be willing to do what it takes to achieve greatness. Which is fine. Just be clear on what you're committing to if you say, "We mean it. Let's go." It's much better not to kid yourselves and freely choose to pretty much stay where you are. The reality may be that you have spent years as a company fighting your way to the middle of the pack and now you just want to rest for a while. No problem. Of course, the inherent danger in that strategy is that there's really no such thing as holding your position. You're either gaining ground or losing ground.

But better to be honestly mediocre and try to stay where you are with a sense of contentment than be unrealistically ambitious about what is yet to be and never get there because you never really wanted to go in the first place. It's demoralizing to any group of people to say year after year that *this* is the year that we go to the mountaintop, when all that ever happens is we just keep on doing what we've been doing with a new set of posters on the walls.

Believe Then Become

Making the decision to go means that you start with an idea and do what's necessary to make the idea a reality. This means that you have to lead with the belief and then follow with action. One without the other won't work. You can't just "believe" your way to becoming extraordinary. You also can't take action that isn't driven by a belief shared within the organization. Action without the foundation of a shared belief usually lacks the power to sustain itself for the amount of time necessary to accomplish something significant.

"We started to tell people that both the employees and the company were the best over and over again until the employees began to believe it," says Larry Morse of Quill. "We highlighted successes and positive comments every time we could so that people would embrace this behavior and action naturally. We began to build a team spirit and purpose toward making Quill the best. Our top-level executives started to build everything around the idea of becoming a high-performance organization and began planning what it would take."

At Quill, they painted a picture of what success would look like for everyone and then began putting the pieces in place. They developed a new and simplified vision statement and then drove home the fact that leadership was the way they were going to bring themselves to the level where they wanted to be. "First," Morse said, "we developed the model of the ideal leader at Quill, which we called *The Quill Leadership Model,* and then taught leadership up and down the organization. Many things were done for effect—for example, putting our logo on everything that moves in order to build team spirit. We focused everyone on one strategic principle: 'We take better care of our customers than anyone else.' To drive it home even further, we created the very 'prestigious' Quill Leadership Institute. As a result, people believe they are the best, they know where we need to go, and they are developing the tools to get there."

CST—Taking It to the Next Level

CST is a professional services company doing business commercially and for the federal government, with a focus primarily on information technology and engineering services. Their government customers fall into two categories: Department of Defense, including the Army, Navy, Air Force, Army Reserve, National Guard, and Corps of Engineers; and civilian agencies, including the Department of Agriculture, Treasury Department, Health and Human Services, Department of Labor, NASA, and Department of Interior.

When CST reached the level of 1,000 employees, they went through an evaluation of where they were and where they wanted to go. This growth threshold was their critical turning point. They wanted to move into doing much bigger contracts and that meant taking the company to the next level. CST president Bobby Bradley says, "You're either growing or you're dying. You've got to continue to grow. If you want to be successful, that's the bottom line. Once you get to 1,000, you've got to look at who you are. Some of the things that got you to 1,000 may not be the same things that get you to the next level."

Remember that old saying: What got you there will seldom keep you there (much less take you to the next level).

CST decided to look at everything, including business development, communications, training, and building the management team for this next level effort. They also determined that they needed to undertake a rebranding process. That was the immediate mission.

Communicating the Vision

Like Quill, CST did much more than just roll out the decision at a big pep rally then go back to business as usual. They followed up with on-going communication about the new CST brand and what it meant to everyone in the company. Donna Bell, corporate communications manager, says, "We made it a big deal. We did a big presentation. We were excited about it. People are going to be interested if they see you're excited. We did have a formal brand rollout process—but it was very personal. We didn't just send out a flashy flyer, although we did start with that. We had our own 'show and tell' mission. We tried to see as many employees as we could face-to-face. Also, we're keeping it going. Little by little, we're communicating our new vision, and our employees are embracing it as we go. So it wasn't just 'here's the new brand, now everybody back to work.' We're talking about a new way of doing business." Bobby Bradley adds, "You get buy-in by being genuine. So that people can trust you and believe in what you say. They have to believe that what you're saying is real and not just fluff."

The Quiet Radical

Sometimes a whisper is much more powerful than a shout. Sometimes taking the time to sit quietly, listen, think, and then discuss will result in much more powerful decisions than the same amount of time spent cheerleading. The quiet gathering is often where the most radical decision making takes place.

I have had the pleasure of working with the Consumer Products Division of Georgia Pacific on a number of occasions. What impresses me most about this organization is the willingness to look at new and even radical ideas in the interest of sparking creative approaches to constant change and improvement.

Everything at their meetings, from the speakers on the agenda to the very setup of the meeting room itself, sets the tone that there is going to be creative thinking taking place. They often bring in outside speakers who present cutting edge ideas designed to blast the cobwebs of stale thinking out of everyone's minds. The general session meeting room is not set up in the traditional classroom or theater style, but instead with a comfortable executive chair and a small side table for each and every participant. The entire atmosphere is one that says, "we mean business." And yet there is an undercurrent of quiet enthusiasm and a vibe of excitement that make the entire event extremely positive for all the participants.

Mike Burandt, president, North American Consumer Products for Georgia Pacific, makes it clear to each of his employees that they are to challenge old ideas, provoke thought, and invite innovation. His consistent message is that everyone's job is to look at his or her company and find a better way to do everything. Mike likes to say that he's looking for crazy ideas, because only ideas that are considered crazy today will be powerful enough to become tomorrow's standards for winning in the marketplace.

Decisions that lead to significant and lasting change in an organization almost always require boldness and courage. Mike Burandt and his team work to create an environment that is supportive of people making courageous decisions.

This isn't change for the sake of change. It certainly isn't change for the sake of following some new business fad or because yet another management guru has written a hot bestseller. It is change in order to find a better way to do what they do, because there's *always* a better way. This Georgia Pacific leadership group is always looking to surprise themselves with innovative ideas and is committed to the decision to follow through. They don't have meetings to talk about greatness. They have meetings to create it.

Talking about It versus Doing It

Some companies think that just because they're having a meeting with the theme "Taking It to the Next Level" means that they're actually doing it. Having a meeting means you're talking about doing it. And the first thing you should talk about is whether or not you truly want to do whatever it is you're saying you want to do. You should look into each other's eyes and ask, "Do we really want to do this? Really?"

Greatness is a decision. It must be chosen. And making that choice is a defining moment in the life of a Category of One company. These defining moments often require courage and audacity, and ultimately involve looking someone straight in the eye and saying something along the lines of "I'm in. Are you?"

Greatness seldom begins because the meeting planning committee picked the right theme or motivational speaker. Greatness begins when people take a deep breath and say, "Well then, let's throw out the way we've been doing it and get on with doing it the way we say we want to do it."

That's where the courage and audacity come in, in that willingness to let go of what used to work in order to clear the space for what will work next. It's one thing to take a vow of progress in a hotel meeting room with 1,000 coworkers in the throes of a motivational feeding frenzy. It's quite another to get back to the office and begin the courageous work of executing strategies that will help ensure that what was talked about and cheered for back in the convention hotel in Cancun will ultimately become reality here in the real world.

Clear Out the Space

Creating processes for change will initially mean throwing old things out more than putting new things in place. You have to clear out the "space" for new ideas to move in. You have to look at your business with new eyes. The decision to go can mean looking at everything you do and simply asking the question "Does this still make sense?"

Once a gut level commitment to go is made, everything changes. If everything doesn't change, then you probably haven't made the commitment. Category of One companies don't tweak, adjust, and tinker. They burn down assumptions and tear apart the way they've always done it. When you commit to becoming extraordinary, things may seem to be in chaos for a while. If you find your company is undertaking a calm, orderly, well-organized transition with the hope of becoming extraordinary, chances are pretty good that you're not making any transition at all. You're just rearranging the furniture. Once you get beyond rearranging furniture, and truly decide to throw the furniture out and move to a new house, then you'll find out who's along for the ride.

This is the part of deciding to go that far too often gets neglected or even ignored completely. The assumption is made that, of course, everyone here is gung-ho to do the things that are being talked about and that it's one for all and all for one. We've all come out of meetings in which decisions were made that, to have any chance of succeeding at all, would require a total team commitment. And yet there are people supposedly a part of that team that everyone knew in their hearts were not committed at all to the decision. They may have even been seriously opposed to it.

That's not to say that a vote has to be taken on every move that a company makes. But it just makes sense that for a company to do extraordinary things and reach new levels of success, at some point, the people involved have to make a commitment. At one time or another each of us has probably been a member of a team that has chosen a course of action with which we disagreed. But most of us have also had the experience of making a total commitment to that course of action, even though we would have preferred another way.

An Hour? A Year? Forever?

Exactly how long does it take to get an entire organization to make the decision to go? Depending on how big the organization is, how well you communicate, the strength of leadership, and many other factors, the answer might be an hour, a week, a year, or never. There are many different scenarios for achieving team commitment, any one of which could apply to your organization.

The size of your organization is a major factor in determining how quickly you can achieve that "critical mass" of commitment necessary to make things begin to happen. A business made up of just a few people can sometimes, though not often, make a significant decision over a pizza in under an hour. Five thousand people will take a little more time. In a perfect world, you'd eventually get a 100 percent commitment from everyone. Everyone in the organization would join the decision to go. The bigger you are, the less likely that's ever going to happen.

You Never Really Get There

For Quill, it became an on-going process. Larry Morse said, "We got in front of employees and repeated our vision over and over again. Communication is the single most important thing we have done. And we backed it up with our training, leadership model, and the establishment of specific goals for the organization. We have rewarded positive behavior and celebrated the successes every step of the way—lots of cake and pizza."

Ultimately, the decision to go becomes a never-ending process for the simple reason that you never get there. The second you achieve success in the marketplace, the marketplace changes, and you have to decide how to win in the new reality. Success is a moving target that causes a very positive version of permanent dissatisfaction. It is a form of dissatisfaction that feels good because you are driven by the fuel of knowing you can do better. It doesn't mean that you don't celebrate your victories. Of course you do. But you also don't rest on yesterday's accomplishments. That's not where the fun is. The fun is in what's next.

Know Who
You Are

Who Are You?

Here's the toughest question that most companies can't answer: Who are you?

When I ask that question of my clients, and I usually do, I'm generally met by one of these responses: "I don't understand the question" or, "We make/sell _____ (fill in the blank with whatever product the company makes/sells)." When met by one of these responses, I'll broaden the parameters of the question a bit. I'll ask them to think about what's important to them, what they're about, what's up with them, what the deal is with them, why they come to work everyday, what good they are in the world, what is meaningful to them about their work, what they're proud of, what they stand for, or what the point of all this activity is.

When given these thought-provoking options, they sometimes still respond with "I don't understand the question." This means trouble. If they have no sense of who they are, what's really important, and what the point of it all is, they are going to find it difficult to compete with a competitor who has got these basics figured out. We're talking about a sense of purpose. Every Category of One company that I've ever worked with has created clarity around the "why" of their business, not just the "what" of their business.

Some companies say that the point is to make money or make a profit. That's like saying that the point of life is to eat. It's backward. Of course you have to eat to stay alive and you have to make a profit to stay in business, but surely eating or making a profit isn't the *point* of it all. Assuming we all agree that making a profit is a good and necessary thing, then perhaps the question to ask is what's the best way for us to go about making a profit.

What's Your Culture?

I did some work with a company whose CEO told me, "We don't really have a culture here. We're more focused on execution than things like culture." I'm sure it's true that they focus more on execution than culture, but I'll guarantee you that this company has a culture as well. Culture is "how we do things around here." Culture is the rules, spoken or unspoken, that you play by. Culture is what you do when the boss is out of town. The question is whether or not you have a culture by design or by accident, and whether the culture you have is the culture you want. Does who you are match your idea of who you want to be?

A Waste of Time?

I worked with a publishing company in Sweden to help them with branding ideas. My approach to branding is that your brand is not your advertising or your logo. Those just help tell the story of the brand. The brand is, in essence, who you are, what you promise, and your ability to deliver on that promise.

I was meeting with the senior leadership team and we were about to launch into an exploration of the question: "Who are you?" About 30 minutes into the discussion, one of the senior vice presidents had had all he could take of me and what he considered to be my rather esoteric and altogether useless search for corporate meaning.

"This whole exercise is a complete waste of our time," he said. He then went on to deliver a spirited rant about they needed to be discussing strategy and execution rather than engaging in an idiotic college philosophy class version of the meaning of life. It was one of those uncomfortable moments in the life of a business consultant. The entire group turned to me waiting for my response. I took a deep breath and said, "Maybe he's right. Maybe we should forget figuring out who you are, what's important, and what you stand for, and go straight to strategy and execution. What do you think?"

One member of the group said, "But how do we even begin to know what our strategy should be if we don't know who we are and what the point of it all is?" With that question the quest for meaning was on. The group began to wrestle with the question of meaning as well as whether it was worthwhile to even ask the question. At the end of the day, the president of the company took me aside and said, "This was the most worthwhile discussion we've had in the 20 years that I've been with this company. We're beginning to tap into something powerful here. We're coming together united behind something bigger than we've ever had."

People with a Common Focus

I'll often ask the question of a group of managers, "How many of you believe that you've got a great team?" Virtually all of them believe that they do have a great team. But a team, by definition, is a group of people with a common focus and a shared purpose or vision—a sense of "who they are." That means that I should be able to approach any member of your team, any employee of your company, and ask them who they are as a team, and get an immediate answer. It should be the easiest question in the world.

But most employees have trouble answering the questions "Who are you?" or "What's important here?" because it never gets talked about. The reality is that it should be being talked about all the time. It's the essence of leadership to constantly remind everybody of who we are and what's important here. Sadly, many people in positions of leadership confuse leadership with management. Management is about how the organization works. Leadership is about why it works and what the point of it all is.

It's Not about the Scoreboard

If we're going to play baseball, a good coach won't say "Okay, team. Get out there and watch that scoreboard!" Spend your time watching the scoreboard and the other team will beat you like a drum. What you've got to do is focus on playing the game and the score will take care of itself. But even beyond the actual mechanics of playing the game, there's got to be a point to it all that will motivate the best possible performance.

The Power of Purpose

I was once speaking to a group of high school students about the idea of giving your work a higher purpose. It wasn't a speech about lofty, philosophical purpose, but rather a very down to earth, practical approach to purpose. During the discussion session after my presentation, the students engaged me in a great question-and-answer exercise about this whole idea of purpose.

One student asked me if I had taken geometry and algebra when I was in high school, to which I responded that yes, I certainly had taken both of those courses, along with chemistry, which I felt might also be included in the question she was about to ask.

She then asked me how I knew what question she was going to ask. I told her that my guess was that she wanted to know if I had ever in my career or life used the information I learned in those classes. Bingo. She said that that was indeed her question.

My response was that no, I didn't recall directly using any of the formulas or principles from geometry, algebra, or chemistry. The student then quite predictably asked what was the point of taking classes in which you learn things that you'll never use. I told her that what I learned to do in those classes was to think. I learned to figure things out using the information that I had at hand. I learned to study and do homework that I absolutely didn't want to do so that I could accomplish my goal, which in my case was not necessarily to be an honors student, but to do the best I could, survive those classes, and get out of there. I told her that the practical value was that every single day in my career and in my life, I have to think and figure things out, and study and do homework that I sometimes don't want to do in order to accomplish my goals. The algebra wasn't the point. For me the point was learning to think.

There were a bunch of guys on the front row who were members of the school's football team. I asked them if they worked out in the gym every day and they all said yes. I then asked them what was the point of, for example, working out with free weights. Was the point of it to become skilled at working with the weights?

"No," they all said. Then what was the point? What was the bigger purpose? What motivated them to go into that gym every day and do something that wasn't all that much fun and was sometimes an absolute drag to do?

One said he worked out to develop certain muscles so that he would be stronger. Another said that he worked out so that he would be more effective in his position on the football team. One of the guys perked up and said the reason he worked out was to get buff so that he could get girls. This was the answer that got an ovation from the entire group. They got the point. And the point was that if we indeed *have* a point to what we do, if we have a purpose bigger than the work itself, we not only will probably do a better job, but we'll create more satisfaction for ourselves in the process.

Boil It Down

Most companies these days have a mission statement, or a vision statement, or both. These are usually carefully crafted missives that say things like we will "be the market leader in providing quality products and services" and "create a superior return for our stakeholders," and "be a positive place for people to work and reach their potential" or other uninspiring corporate-speak that means little or nothing to anyone in the real world. It's nice to have a mission statement. It's necessary to have a mission statement. But what's the point of the mission statement if not to get to the guts of what we're all about in a way that actually means something significant, personal, and *exciting* to the people in the organization?

I was working with a company that provides medical services through walk-in centers throughout the country. Early in their meeting, they had put the company mission statement on a screen during the president's presentation. It a typical, bland, expected, nice, neat, mission statement. During my presentation, I asked the group if anyone could tell me what their mission statement really meant. There were no takers. In fact, most of the group immediately went into advanced eye contact avoidance techniques to avoid being called on.

I changed the question a bit. I said to imagine that I had just met them at a party and was curious about their company. What would they tell me was the essence of what their company was all about? Still no response.

I picked one woman sitting on the end of a row and told her to just boil down that mission statement to what it really meant to her. She said, "You're obviously looking for some particular answer and I don't know what you want me to say." I assured her that I just wanted to know what the mission statement meant to her and that there was no wrong answer. She stuck to her guns and refused to answer. I then upped the challenge by saying that I didn't understand how she could be a manager in a company for years and have absolutely no sense of what the mission statement meant. I said, "Just tell me what your company does that means anything to anybody!"

In a now clearly agitated and almost angry voice, the woman rose out of her chair, looked me right in the eyes, and said "WE HELP PEOPLE WHEN THEY'RE HURT, OKAY!!!" Woof. Now we're talking. From meaningless mission statement to something powerful that came straight from the gut. There's a big difference between an intellectual understanding of what business you are in and a gut level understanding of what the point of it all is.

I asked the group how many of them knew the mission statement and felt that it was a motivator that gave them a reason to get up in the morning and charge in to work ready to take on the world. None of them raised their hands. I then asked how many of them felt that "helping people when they're hurt" was something that they could really get behind and be motivated about. It was unanimous. Everyone in the room, including the president of the company, raised their hands. "Well, there you go," I said. "Now you've got a mission with some power behind it."

Strong Language

A weakness of so many companies is their reluctance to use powerful language to express what they claim are powerful ideas. Sometimes people in business are so afraid of being "inappropriate" that they get stuck in using bland, flavorless corporate-speak that accomplishes absolutely nothing.

It happens all the time. A group of executives go off to some resort with a consultant for three days to come up with a mission statement that will be the foundation for everything that they want to accomplish. What they do is slowly squeeze the life out of their words until they end up with some tepid statement about being the market leader and providing a good return for their shareholders. Good grief!

What's really inappropriate is having a mission or vision statement that means absolutely nothing to anyone. What purpose does a mission statement serve if no one gets excited about it? Now that's inappropriate. If you have strong feelings about your company, your people, your customers, and your work, then use *strong* language.

I was in a meeting recently in which the company had put the various elements of their vision statement on the walls around the conference room. I loved one of the statements in particular. It read: "We hate bureaucracy and all the nonsense that comes with it. We will kill red tape wherever we find it." Now you're talking. They could have said something along the lines of "In the interest of becoming a more efficient and effective organization, we will constantly strive to improve our processes and procedures." How utterly, completely emotionless. And it would have elicited an emotionless response that would have accomplished nothing.

Another example of strong and effective language is part of a mission statement I saw that read: "If you're as good as you're going to get then find another place to work."

They could have said something about "constant improvement" or "reaching our potential as individuals." Neither of those bloodless statements would have had the power of "If you're as good as you're going to get then find another place to work." There is no part of that statement that I don't understand. It works because it's strong language expressing a powerful idea.

Vision versus Product

One of my favorite companies is LensCrafters. I've been doing consulting work with them for years, and they've been selling me eyeglasses for years. But to say that they just sell me eyeglasses wouldn't be their version of the transaction. They would say that they help me see better. What's the difference? Plenty.

With hundreds of stores in the United States and Canada, LensCrafters is an industry leader in the highly competitive optical retail market. LensCrafters is an indirect, wholly owned subsidiary of Luxottica Group, S.p.A., an Italy-based market leader in the design, manufacturing, and marketing of mid- to premium-eyeglass frames and sunglasses.

If you were asked to say what business LensCrafters is in, it would be reasonable if you said that they are in retail sales. They have stores, often in shopping malls, that sell eyeglasses. The question for LensCrafters is: Would being a retail sales organization best serve them, their customers, and the world? To get right down to the business bottom line, would being a retail sales organization be the best way for them to make money?

I can't speak to what motivates LensCrafters to look at their business the way they do, but from an outsider's perspective as one of their business partners and as a customer, I can certainly attest to the effectiveness of their particular vision of who they are, what they stand for, and what the point of it all is. LensCrafters has achieved that sometimes elusive but always powerful goal of boiling down what they do to a gut level. It's that clearly understood and genuinely felt statement of purpose that turns their people on.

The LensCrafters vision is, quite simply: "We will be the best at helping the world see better." There's a very practical business element to this vision. They say that they will be the best by "creating customers for life by delivering legendary customer service, developing and energizing associates and leaders in the world's best workplace, crafting perfect-quality eyewear in about an hour, and delivering superior overall value to meet each customer's individual needs."

LensCrafters further says that they will "help the world see by . . . being conveniently available to people everywhere, ensuring people think of us as the first choice for eye care, serving more people in our markets than all other optical retailers do combined, and *giving the gift of sight to those who have the least and need us the most.*"

That's where LensCrafters' real power is, in that last statement of purpose: "giving the gift of sight to those who have the least and need us the most." This is the switch that turns their people on. This is where they become more than what they sell. They have a purpose much bigger than product sales.

LensCrafters says they believe that good vision is a basic human right, not a luxury. In 1988, they created Give the Gift of Sight, a charitable program that has helped more than two million underprivileged people see clearly in the United States and in 25 developing countries around the world. LensCrafters doctors and associates work with Lions Club International to collect and recycle old glasses, execute optical missions in developing countries, offer vision screenings at health fairs, and provide new glasses to preselected needy people in their stores and their two mobile Vision Vans. By the time this book is published, LensCrafter's goal is to give the gift of sight to three million people around the world.

This is all well and good and surely a most worthy cause. But many companies participate in worthwhile charitable efforts and do good works for their community. To be a good corporate citizen of the community is pretty much expected these days. What's so special about what LensCrafters is doing? The answer to that can be found in the attitude of the people at LensCrafters and their whole approach to what they do.

I Get That Smile

Of the half million Gift of Sight recipients helped each year, the majority are served in local nursing homes, homeless shelters, and inner-city schools. Gift of Sight OutReach allows LensCrafters volunteers to go into their communities to reach those who do not have access to eye care.

Volunteers visit nursing homes and shelters to find many residents wearing glasses that no longer fit as originally intended. After years of wear, glasses may affect the way a person can—or cannot see.

The payoff for correcting these kinds of problems was expressed by one LensCrafters' manager who said "There are people at every nursing home who need more than an eyeglass adjustment—what they really need is a smile. I choose to serve others through the Gift of Sight program to get that smile for myself."

We Help People See Better

I've been fortunate enough to participate in a number of LensCrafters meetings across the country, including their big annual manager's convention. Like most corporate meetings, this event is held in an appropriately exciting location in a big convention hotel with all the trappings you'd expect of a major corporate function. It's a first-class program from start to finish.

What most impressed me at one particular manager's convention, however, was the opening general session. Frank

Baynham, executive vice president, Stores, Luxottica Retail, opened the meeting with an address to his managers that I can best sum up in four words, "Remember who we are." I don't recall anything being said about sales or revenue or profit in his opening address. His speech was about all those things that far too many companies don't ever think about. Things like who we are, what's important, and what's the point. The numbers he talked about were the number of people that LensCrafters had helped to see better.

Frank's speech was followed by two video presentations. One told the story of a LensCrafters customer who had left San Francisco with his family on a flight to JFK airport in New York, where they would transfer to their flight to Europe for a two-week vacation. Shortly after leaving San Francisco, the customer dropped his glasses and they were stepped on and broken beyond any possible use.

Taking a chance on what the customer said was "the longest of long shots," he used the telephone on the plane to call his LensCrafters back in San Francisco, told them about what had happened, and asked if there was anything at all that they could suggest.

The LensCrafters employee told him that they'd try and come up with something. What they came up with was that when the customer stepped off the plane in New York, a Long Island, New York, LensCrafters employee met him at the gate with a new pair of glasses with the customer's prescription.

At the end of the video, the crowd of managers went absolutely ballistic. The cheering was loud and long and there was no doubt that this story was a vivid reminder of the essence of "who they are"—they help the world see better. If LensCrafters was just in the retail business of selling eyeglasses, there's a possibility that this story would have turned out just the same. But having a purpose beyond selling a product, a purpose to help people see better, was a point of pride and motivation that quite probably made something extraordinary happen. It calls to mind the movie *The Blues Brothers.* Remember what helped them overcome each and every obstacle to raising the money and paying the taxes to save the orphanage? "We're on a mission from God."

The second video shown at that opening general session told the story of a prematurely born baby, not expected to live beyond a few days, one of whose health complications was a serious vision problem. The local LensCrafters was contacted about the situation, and worked with the baby's physicians to craft a tiny pair of glasses for the child. In the video, the parents of the baby said she had clearly been able to see much better with those specially made glasses. The baby's father wrote that they were so thankful that their child had been able to clearly see her mother and father before she passed away.

As you might expect, the entire convention hall was silent at the conclusion of this video, with quiet crying the only sound. This video wasn't meant to be a tearjerker for the sake of drumming up emotion. It got to the core of the LensCrafters message: Remember who we are, we help the world see better.

On my flight back home from the meeting, I sat next to a LensCrafters store manager. In discussing his job and why he loved it so much, he said something that struck me as particularly significant. He said, "I always knew I'd end up in health care and help people. I thought that maybe I'd be a doctor or a dentist, but I'm so happy I ended up with LensCrafters helping people with their sight." This LensCrafters manager didn't see himself as being the manager of a retail store in a mall. He saw himself as being in health care, helping people with their sight. Extraordinary.

A Gift of Insight

One Lenscrafters manager who has participated extensively expressed her commitment to the Gift of Sight program by saying, "I feel the Gift of Sight is more than a privilege. It is my duty. It is truly a blessing to work with local organizations to help the neediest in our community."

A LensCrafters optician feels that she is the one who benefits from the Gift of Sight program. "I received the gift of sight, today, the only difference is that mine was a gift of *insight*," she said. "There's nothing more beautiful than the face of a little girl when she looks up and sees the hands of a clock for the first time—or the man who can now complete a job application because of his new glasses."

Some ideas, like the notion of your job being much more than just a job, become meaningless clichés. At LensCrafters, they have taken their jobs and made them life missions that bring meaning to everything they do. They know who they are.

Remember Who You Are

An executive of a telecommunications company once told me that his father placed a great deal of importance in the idea of knowing who you are. He said that his father would tell him and his brothers and sisters stories about his grandparents and great-grandparents and the family values that had been passed along through the generations. These values were such rock solid principles as honesty, integrity, and being a gentleman or lady at all times. By the time he reached his teens, there was no doubt about who he was and what it meant to be a member of this family.

The problem though, he said, was that this whole business of remembering who you are got in the way of what he thought would be a lot of fun. He said that when he got his driver's license he looked forward with great mischievous anticipation to his first Saturday night out on the streets in his dad's car. He had great visions of the fun and trouble that a guy with four wheels could get into. As he walked out the front door for his big night out, his father looked up from his newspaper and said, "Have a good time out there tonight. And son, remember who you are."

Well, of course, it was the "remember who you are" that took the steam out of all his rambunctious plans to wreak havoc and raise hell across the countryside. He told me that his father had done such a great job of instilling a sense of purpose and identity into all of the kids, that all they had to do to know how to behave was go back to that touchstone of remembering who they were.

Decisions in Advance

When a company knows who it is and what's really important, it's a great compass and timesaver when it comes to decision making. Organizations that don't really have a sense of purpose have to pretty much start at ground zero when faced with a strategic decision of almost any kind. It's like that old saying, "If you don't know where you're going, pretty much any road will get you there." The same holds true here. If you don't know who you are, how do you know what decision to make?

A companywide sense of purpose and identity makes decision making easier and more efficient. It's certainly true for individuals. There's a great scene from the movie *Moonstruck* that illustrates how knowing who you are can make a decision easy to make. A chance meeting in a restaurant has resulted in a friendship springing up between the characters Perry and Rose. In front of Rose's house, after Perry has walked her home, this exchange takes place:

Perry: "I guess you can't invite me in."
Rose: "No."
Perry: "People home?"
Rose: "No. The house is empty. I can't invite you in because
   I'm married. Because I know who I am."

How do you know what to do when faced with a difficult decision? You want to do the right thing but how do you know what that is? My friend Phil Van Hooser teaches the concept of making decisions in advance.

Phil, who once aspired to become a professional baseball umpire, says that the key to being a good umpire is in calling the pitches consistently. The umpire must position himself behind the plate in such a way that he calls the pitches the same way every time.

This same principle works in our everyday lives and businesses. You position yourself in advance so that when difficult questions come up, you don't have to wrestle with the answer. You've answered the tough questions in advance.

In my own business, one decision made in advance that made my life much simpler was that I was no longer going to accept after-dinner speaking engagements. I didn't like doing them and I wasn't particularly good at it. But if I decided on a case-by-case basis it was too tempting to justify taking the job because of the money. But by deciding in advance, there's no decision to make—the decision has already been made.

Often an extraordinary company stays focused because they have decided in advance what businesses they do not want to be in or what kinds of customers they do not want to work with. All of this goes back to creating clarity around who you are and what the point is. That's how the whole business of goal setting works. Some people say they don't believe in setting goals. That it's all mumbo jumbo. They're missing the point.

Goal setting works like this: I decide that I want to white-water raft down the Colorado River next year. I remind myself every day that this is a goal. Over the course of the year I resist the temptation to buy stuff because I know that what I want the most is to raft the Colorado and that's what I'm saving my money for.

Day-to-day decisions become much easier when you've given thought to what's important and what you're all about. For example, you could go to the business meeting but you've decided in advance that you will never again miss another of your daughter's birthdays. Or you could accept that financially lucrative contract but it would mean working with idiots and you've decided in advance that you won't work with idiots.

You could hire the lone wolf top performer but you've decided in advance that you want to hire only team players.

Do I Want to Work with You?

Every company faces the never-ending challenge of attracting and retaining good employees. The whole issue of hiring good people is directly tied to the issue of being more than the product that you sell. In a marketplace where everyone is competing for scarce talent and the best and brightest people, you must have a clear sense of who you are so that you can attract the people you want. Employer branding is as important as being branded with customers. They both want to know who you are. If *you* don't know, how in the world are *they* supposed to know?

The necessity for differentiating your company as an employer is the same as it is with customers. But most companies don't differentiate at all. They go to the employment marketplace with generic statements like "We're a great place to work." Well, that doesn't really give me much information, does it? I don't have a particularly clear sense of what it's like to work with you at this point, do I? And it doesn't help much to list such "specific" advantages as good pay, regular vacations, excellent benefits, and good advancement opportunities. You're offering the same thing that any prospective employer offers.

For me to want to work for you, I have to know *what it's like* to work for you.

Southwest Airlines, in their quest for the right people to be flight attendants, has run a print ad that features a photo taken through a window of one of their planes in flight, looking out over a beautiful, clear blue sky. The headline of the ad says, "Does Your Current Job Have a View Like This?" The copy goes on to say "We're looking for unique people interested in a rewarding career as Southwest Airlines Flight Attendants. You'll receive outstanding benefits, travel privileges, and the power to express yourself while being part of a company renowned for its fun, supportive culture. If you're interested in a job where your career is what you make of it, simply create and submit your resume online at southwest.com."

Parts of that recruitment ad cover the expected bases. There's nothing particularly revealing about offering "outstanding benefits" or "travel privileges" if you're an airline. Where Southwest appeals to the heart of prospective employees is when it talks about "the power to express yourself" and a "fun, supportive culture."

There's even a subtle message in the invitation to "create" your resume. Anyone who has flown Southwest knows that its flight attendants are most definitely encouraged to express themselves, and the culture is certainly fun.

The problem with most business leaders is that they're scared to death of words that really mean something. They'd rather stay within the nice, neat, and, above all, safe confines of traditional vanilla corporate language that doesn't say anything truly meaningful. Actually, most business leaders prefer numbers. You can get your arms around numbers. You can quantify with numbers. You can make charts and graphs with numbers. But you can't reach anybody emotionally with numbers. And that's the inherent weakness of numbers.

Dreams—Not Strategic Plans

Once you decide what your company is all about—what's important, what the point is—then you must use language that conveys that message with feeling. I know what your product is, but *what's it like* to work for you? It could well be that the essence of who you are and what it's like is that you are focused on making the finest products of their kind in the world. You may be looking for people who get turned on by striving for technical perfection in the interest of making a quality product that performs a significant function in the world. Then say so and you'll attract the people you want. What's significant to me might not be significant at all to you and vice versa. The point is that you want to get people on your team that share the same vision. We're not talking about clones or people with identical personalities. But people who will share a common vision and purpose.

In his speech in 1963, the Reverend Martin Luther King Jr. didn't rally thousands of people to the cause of civil rights with his "I Have a Strategic Plan" speech. It was his "I Have a Dream" speech. Strategic plans are good and necessary things, and without execution, dreams are just hallucinations. But what best determines effective strategic plans and what most effectively fuels the execution of those plans is people who are working to make their dreams come true.

So what's your company like? I have to know if I'm going to want to work there. If it's a cool place to work then say so. One client of mine is a leader in the business of making e-commerce systems work. They say that they are young, risk-taking, extremely good at what they do, and even a little bit cocky about it. That's going to attract a certain kind of employee. The exact kind they're looking for. What if they put the word out that they were a "great place to work with good benefits and excellent chances for advancement?" It's a cookie-cutter statement that would attract cookie-cutter people. They'd be disappointed with the results and would probably wonder why they couldn't find the right people to fit their team.

Greatness attracts greatness. As Bobby Bradley of CST said, "I've always had the objective of being a great company. We've concentrated on being a great company because of our people and having THEM feel like it's a great company. Our culture is also key. If you have a great culture, you get the great people—and the other stuff will come. People are attracted to that dream or vision and it's perpetuated through the people. And that's a great company. The growth will come. The revenue will come. The relationships with the customer will come."

Good Guys or Bad Guys?

Today's customer, whether a retail consumer or a business-to-business buyer, is very different from the customer of even just a few years ago. We used to make buying decisions based pretty much on product, price, and service. That was it. Give me a good product at a competitive price with good service and you win my business. Today, there's a whole new component in the customer's decision-making process. Are you a good guy or a bad guy?

With the combination of access to more information than ever before along with a heightened social and political consciousness, today's customer wants to know who you are before she buys your product. She wants to know, and does know, what political candidates your company supports, what social causes you are involved in, what contribution you make to the community, whether or not you are environmentally responsible, how you treat your employees, and if the people who run your company are honest.

Because of past sins, real or perceived, customers will refuse to do business with certain retail chains, gas stations, clothing manufacturers, banks, and just about any other kind of business you can think of. You can have the greatest product of its kind on the planet, but if the customer thinks that who you are is one of the bad guys, you won't get their business.

I Want Them to Succeed

I think that I'm pretty much like most people in that whether in the movies, or in sports, or in business, I want the good guys to win. I want extraordinary companies that stand for something more than making money to succeed. What qualifies some companies for Category of One status in the marketplace isn't necessarily product or price or service at all. It could be that they are competitive in those areas, but hold no particular advantage over their competitors there. It could be that customers perceive them as being a company of substance that truly does something good in the world.

I am an unabashed fan of LensCrafters for a lot of reasons, but mostly because I like who they are. I want them to succeed. When I walk into my LensCrafters store in the Green Hills Mall in Nashville, Tennessee, the first thing I see is that big barrel where they ask customers to donate their used glasses. I know that those glasses become part of the Give the Gift of Sight program, and make their way to countries all over the world to help LensCrafters *give the gift of sight to those who have the least and need us the most.*

Does LensCrafters sell a good product? I think so. Is it the best product available? Quite frankly, I don't know. Do they have the best price? I wouldn't know. I'm assuming that they're competitive. Do they give the best service? My personal experience has been that they give great service. I believe the key to that service goes full circle right back to that toughest question that most companies can't answer: Who are you? LensCrafters works hard at answering that question every day and I believe it's been the key to their success.

LensCrafters has never gone out of their way to publicize their Give the Gift of Sight program, and that in itself speaks volumes about who they are. They don't say "buy your glasses from us because we are good guys." They do what they do because they really can't do it any other way. It's not a policy; it's an identity. Helping people see better isn't their job; it's what they have to do because of who they are.

This, then, becomes the real test of whether your company has a true sense of identity as opposed to just having a policy. If you do good work because it's in the company manual, it's a policy. If you do good work because you don't know any other way to do it, it's your identity.

It's Just What We Do Here

I was staying at the Four Seasons Hotel in downtown Atlanta to speak at a client meeting on branding. Anyone who has stayed in any Four Seasons Hotel will probably agree with me that this is truly a fine brand. They are beautiful properties staffed with people who give really great service. At this particular Four Seasons, however, I learned how their sense of who they are resulted in true Category of One status.

With a couple of hours to kill until I joined my client's meeting, I took my luggage to the lobby, checked my bags for brief storage with a hotel bellman, and took a seat on one of the lobby couches to do some work. I spread my files and papers out on the table in front of me and went to work. After about 15 minutes, the young bellman who had checked my bags approached me and said "Mr. Calloway (he had obviously spotted my name on one of my luggage tags), it looks like you're dug in here for a while, right?" "Yes," I said, "I'm going to be working here for probably another 90 minutes or so. Why do you ask?" "Well," he said, "We've got a pitcher of peach iced tea over there and I was thinking that I might bring a glass over here for you." "Great idea," I said.

As he went to get the tea, I started thinking about what was going on, and when he returned with the tea I asked, "Say, this might sound like a funny question, but why did you do that?" "Do what?" he asked. "You mean why did I get you the iced tea?" "Yes. What made you think of doing that?" I asked. "Is that in your training?" He looked at me with a bit of a puzzled look on his face and said, "Well, Mr. Calloway, we get training all the time here. But it's not really part of the training to get tea for someone. I guess you'd say it's just what we do here. It just seemed to me that you might enjoy it."

When you transcend policy, you begin to transcend commodity. Well, you might be thinking, a Four Seasons Hotel isn't exactly a commodity. Sure it is. When compared with their usual competitors, like Ritz Carlton or Preferred Hotels, or Trump International Hotel in New York City, they're all a commodity at a very high level. And at that level, you have to differentiate with more than product, price, and service. You have to differentiate with who you are.

The One Thing

If I were asked to identify the one thing that virtually all Category of One companies have in common, it would be that they talk about the same things over and over. This is how cultures are created. You decide what's important, then you talk about it. Over and over. And over. For years. Repetition is the mother of a strong corporate culture.

Companies that have no sense of who they are or what they stand for will have a different theme for each year's annual meeting, a constantly changing set of priorities, and no real foundation to depend on during times of change. Extraordinary companies are, in one sense, incredibly boring. They are always talking about the same thing. It's such a simple idea that many people reject it out of hand. Decide what's important and talk about it all the time. It's not a sexy idea. It just works.

One Trick Ponies

I believe that great leaders are creative, innovative, and always looking for ways to improve their organizations. I also believe that great leaders are "one trick ponies." When it comes down to what really counts, they don't have a lot of changing ideas. They stick with what's important and they talk about it over and over and over. Remember, leaders remind us of who we are.

Beyond Survival

Over the past few years, I personally feel that words like "passion" might have been used a little too lightly in terms of why we work. But I do believe very strongly that for a company, or even an individual, to achieve a sustained level of high performance, there must be a point to their work that goes beyond survival.

I don't believe that for a company to succeed it must be filled with wild-eyed zealots who consider themselves to be on a life or death crusade to save the world. What seems to work in the real world isn't the "over-the-top" version of commitment, which usually burns out like a comet that has a brief run across the night sky. What seems to work is a quieter, deeper commitment like that felt in the hearts and minds of LensCrafters employees. They aren't necessarily trying to save the world. They're trying to help people see better.

To me, that kind of sense of commitment to a purpose greater than self-interest is the most motivating and useful answer to the question, "Who are you?" George Bernard Shaw put it this way when he wrote, "This is the true joy in life, being used for a purpose recognized by yourself as a mighty one. Being thoroughly used up and worn out before you are thrown on the scrap heap. Being a force of nature instead of a feverish, selfish little clod of ailments and grievances complaining that the world will not devote itself to making you happy."

Success Means You Know What *Used* to Work

Change Is Good—You Go First

The way you used to do it won't work much longer. It's not because you're necessarily doing anything wrong, it's just that everything about the way we do business is changing. It's changing now, as you read this. And it's going to keep on changing.

Intellectually, everyone agrees that change is a good and necessary thing. However, most of us are, to at least some extent, resistant to change. We don't like it. We aren't comfortable with it. It scares us. Most people would say, "Change is good. You go first."

A few years ago, people were riding through the corporate countryside like Paul Revere, shouting, "The Internet is here! The Web changed everything!" And so it did. Just like the telegraph did, the railroad did, the internal combustion engine did, the assembly line did, television did, and computers did. What's significant now is not the Internet, particularly, but the speed at which changes are cascading down around us in a constant flow that never lets up and, in fact, increases in speed all the time.

From shifts in the economy that put buyers in control of the marketplace, to the staggering number of new technologies, to changes in how we live and what employees want from their companies—big changes are everywhere. Big changes aren't new. We've always had them and always will. But big changes that come at you at light speed in a never-ending stream—that's new. Change today is constant, sudden, and significant.

It's become a challenge to even define what business you're in anymore. When the differences between insurance companies, banks, and stock brokers begin to fade into a kind of oneness, they are all in the same business: financial services. New competitors are everywhere for everybody. People go to the grocery store to open a checking account. They go to the Internet to find a second mortgage. They buy a Cadillac because they're a fan of the Bose stereo equipment in the car. The lines are blurring and new rules of competition are being written everyday.

Past Success Is the Enemy

Past success can be, and usually is, the enemy of future success. This is a rule that I live by in my own business. What it means is simply that if you have a track record of past success, and you are good at what you do, then I would say two things to you.

The first is to offer my sincere congratulations. I am a firm believer in celebrating our successes and recognizing great achievements.

The second thing I would say is that you have put yourself in a very dangerous position. When a company or an individual becomes successful, they inevitably experience the pull of an almost irresistible force—complacency. The greatest danger of past success is that you might relax into thinking that you "know how this business works." Every successful company must be on guard against the threat of complacency. You have to create a sense of urgency every day in *every* thing you do.

My own company has been fortunate enough to experience consistent success in the 20-plus years that we've been in business, and for that we are endlessly thankful. It is because of that success that every day I say to myself, "Calloway, if you're successful, that means you know what *used to work*. If you're successful, that means that you can compete and win in markets that *no longer exist*. They're gone. The game starts over today and it will start over again tomorrow."

I'm not saying that you should throw out everything you've done to make your company successful. Far from it. There are things you did yesterday and maybe for as long as you've been in business that will work tomorrow and possibly forever. These tend to be in the areas of basic values like integrity, creating mutually beneficial relationships with customers and employees, and providing honest value. What I am saying is don't make assumptions about what will work tomorrow based on what worked yesterday, especially in the area of processes, procedures, strategies, and operations.

One good model for maintaining forward movement, while creating the stability that comes from a solid foundation, is to think of your company as having a solid, stable core. Imagine that your company is designed like the planet Saturn, with the core planet surrounded by rings. The core represents your values, what's important, who you are, and what you stand for. This rarely changes and can serve you well, assuming you've chosen a good set of values, for as long as you are in business.

But think of the rings that surround your company as the way you do business in terms of tactics. These rings change constantly, just as products, society, technology, economies, and customers do. Always remember who you are and what you stand for, but also look at how you must change to meet the needs of a world that is new every single day.

Prosperity can be very dangerous for any company. It can lead you to believe that you've "cracked the code," or "figured this business out," or that you "know how this business works." No. You know how it *used* to work. To stop and relax for more than a brief moment is one of the most dangerous things you can do in a marketplace that changes constantly. This doesn't mean that you should run scared or operate your business in a panic mode. In fact, the companies that tend to operate most confidently are those that are comfortable with constant change, thus avoiding the desperate game of "catch up" that has to be played when complacency has frozen you into inaction.

Big Changes? Little Changes?

For years, the prevailing school of thought was that to create quality in an organization, you should undertake a strategy of constant, small improvements in all areas. It was a linear approach that sought ways to make improvements in what you were already doing. How can we cut costs? How can we reduce the time it takes to fulfill a customer's order? It was the "sharpen the blade of the axe so that we can chop down more trees" approach to business. That's fine as far as it goes, and I'm certainly a fan of tweaking when need be.

But the problem with thinking only in terms of constant, small improvements is that it can blind you to looking above the day-to-day fray, seeing a bigger picture, and making huge, monster improvements that come through the complete reinvention of something. Instead of sharpening the blade of the axe, maybe we should see if there's a better way to chop down trees in the first place. Come to think of it, maybe chopping down trees isn't even the business we should be in. Let's stop looking at how to improve what we're doing and take a look at what we're doing in the first place.

It's good to improve something 10 percent. It's also really, really good to improve something 500 percent. Or to invent something totally new and change the rules of the game altogether. The goal used to be achieving growth by getting better at what you were already doing. Now an additional goal is to be ready to adapt, immediately, to the next thing that you'll need to be doing.

This isn't about change just for the sake of change. Changing just for the sake of changing can be a more dangerous trap than being stuck in complacency. The graveyard of failed businesses is full of companies that were willing to try anything, whether it made sense or not, just so they could feel like they were "riding the waves of change."

It became quite popular in the go-go days of the Internet boom for business gurus to say that in the "new economy" you had to create chaos and throw everything out to have a chance at survival in the brave new world of e-commerce. That approach didn't exactly pan out, either. There's absolutely nothing wrong with a little chaos now and then. In fact, it's healthy, particularly if your business is at a turning point in its history.

Somebody's Got to Buy Something

But some rules of doing business can't be thrown away. The notion, for example, that a business has to actually sell something to someone at some point to survive has proven to be a pretty tenacious law of commerce. Hundreds of failed Internet companies discovered that. Besides, there's no new economy anyway. There never was one. There was the Internet trying to find it's place in the existing economy—period. Which it still is.

Just because it's a brand new idea doesn't mean that it's a better idea. It's like believing that if you "follow your bliss" you'll be financially successful. That's only true if somebody out there is interested in buying what following your bliss produces. You can follow your bliss and pursue your passion all day long, but if you're not very good at it, or if there's no market for it, it won't work. Lots of start-ups thought that somehow if they just had fun and came up with swell ideas and threw nerf balls and had pizza parties in the office and were generally cool, that they'd make money. New doesn't always mean better. At some point, somebody's got to buy something.

Outside-the-Box Lip Service

One of the most popular and vastly overused business phrases of our time is think "outside the box." I've probably heard those words used a thousand times at business meetings and conventions over the past 10 years. It's usually pure lip service. We love to talk about innovation, but the reality of it tends to scare most people to death. "I like change. Change it back the way it was." seems to be the change mantra for most people.

Of course, staying in the box isn't safe at all. The biggest risk is to never take one. If you think change is scary, try not changing. Not changing is the scariest strategy of all in a world of constant change. It would be like being a fish in the ocean saying, "I don't like all this water." Change is just like the water, you're surrounded by it, get used to it. Better yet, learn to thrive in it.

More and more companies are starting to ask really big, scary questions like "Are we even in the right business?" and "What's happening *outside* our industry that we can learn from?" Evolving Category of One companies are not only willing, but also anxious, to look at businesses totally different from their own in the quest for what they might do next. Mediocre companies are the ones that always rally around the flag of "but that's just not done in this business." It's just not done until a competitor does it and you end up wondering where all your customers went.

Another way of getting out of your box is to invite people from a totally different box to come in and join you. When Quill decided to take the company to a significantly higher level, they knew that it would take some new blood to help them get there. The management team at Quill had done a great job of running the company as it was, but it would take a different set of skills and a new perspective to make Quill the company they wanted it to be.

The introduction of new blood and new ideas into a company will usually cause some initial discomfort. There's always a level of tension that's part of the process of change in a company. When old ideas come up against new ones, and when the status quo comes up against a new goal, it's not always an easy thing to work through. But if everyone in the company is happy and comfortable with the pace and the degree of change that's taking place, you can be pretty sure that there's nothing really serious going on. It's a natural law that people have to get riled up for something big to happen.

True out-of-the-box companies also work to mix people from different departments, with different job titles, and totally different views of the company and what it's about. In most corporate meetings, you'll see the human resources people sitting together and the information technology people sitting together, and so on. Mix them up. And not just to sit together in silence while the department heads speak. Give them a chance to talk with one another and discuss their respective jobs and points of view within the company. What you want is to get opinions, perceptions, ideas, and issues to move across boundaries. Do some cross training and teach people what the other people in your company do. Shake up the box and see what ideas fall out.

Stability through Change

For a very long time, one of the measures of stability in a company was its rate of change. The less it changed, the more stable it was perceived to be, and rightly so. Until fairly recently, we could predict the future reasonably well, and for quite a distance out.

Companies didn't need to change so much because the world around them didn't change very much.

We've always had changes. That's nothing new. And we've always had big, momentous changes that redefined everything. You could make a case that the impact of the telegraph was in many ways as significant in its time as the impact of the Internet in our time. The railroad, the assembly line, the telephone, the airplane, the computer—all were monumental in the impact that they had on life and business.

The big difference now is that major changes don't happen occasionally, they happen all the time. It's infinitely more difficult to see them coming. That means that not only does a company have to be willing to change and change often, it has to be willing to be wrong. The one thing you know for sure today if you forecast is that you're going to be wrong. That doesn't mean you shouldn't forecast, it simply means that instead of success being based on always making the right decision or prediction, success is based on being able to move quickly from one decision to the next. Even if you're right, you are still going to have to move on in a very short period of time.

Things change so constantly that by the time we analyze a situation and figure out what's going on, the situation itself has changed. So analysis of what's going on can't take place periodically, it has to happen all the time. And our response to and anticipation of what's happening also becomes continuous.

Today if a company doesn't change, not only is it most likely not stable, it is at serious risk of disappearing altogether. Remember that we're talking about tactics and operations, not values. A foundation of values surrounded by those flexible rings of changeable tactics is the strongest basis for stability in business today. You can most successfully change what you're doing and how you do it if you have a clear sense of who you are.

Movement is a stabilizing factor today. Companies today are like bicyclists who have their feet permanently strapped into the pedals. They can't stop and put their feet down anymore like they used to. They have to keep moving or they will fall. That's why a crisis is often a good thing for a company. A crisis can force you to eliminate ways of doing business that don't work anymore. A crisis can force necessary movement.

The Invisible Fence

Looking back over my own career, it's clear that some of the most significant periods of progress that I experienced were caused by what seemed at the time like crisis, not opportunity. I had fallen prey to relaxing because my business was experiencing success, customers were happy, and I could see absolutely no reason to do anything other than what was already working. It was as if someone had installed one of those invisible fences around me, like you would use to train your pet not to wander away from your yard. My invisible fence was made up of the boundaries that complacency had erected in my mind. I thought I was safe because nothing was changing. In fact, I had made myself vulnerable to the inevitable change in the marketplace that I chose to ignore.

In the mid–eighties, about 75 percent of my business was coming from two clients, a regional bank and the U.S. Army. I had been doing marketing work for both of these clients for a few years, they were absolutely happy, and there was no apparent reason for anything to change in the foreseeable future. I felt secure in the belief that if I kept doing a good job at doing what I had been doing, tweaking and making small

improvements along the way, that my business would continue to thrive and steadily grow.

Two things happened almost simultaneously that turned
my safe little world upside down. Because of some acquisitions
and fundamental shifts in strategy by my bank client, they went
through the process of some serious budget cutting. The por-
tion of the budget that paid for me was one of the casualties.
They said, "We love you. We'll hire you again someday. But
right now we're cutting all programs like yours. Good luck and
goodbye."

At about the same time, the general who was in charge of
my program was transferred. His replacement summoned me
to his headquarters and began by saying, "We love you. You've
done a great job for the Army. If you were my guy I'd keep
you. But you're not my guy. And the way it works is that the
outgoing general's guys go away and the new general's guys
come in. Good luck and goodbye."

Doom, gloom, and despair settled around me like a cloud
and I was having trouble seeing any silver lining. Everything
had changed and it was difficult for me to see the opportunity
from 75 percent of my business disappearing. My first order of
business was to survive until I could figure out my next move.

To create some cash flow, I sought out and found some
clients for short-term consulting and training programs. At the
same time, I began to pursue opportunities as a business speaker
for corporate conventions and meetings. What I quickly discovered was that the pricing for these shorter term services was
totally different than for the type of consulting I had been
doing. The bottom line result was that I ended up making
much more money per day with a much larger base of clients
with the bonus of doing work that I found more stimulating

and satisfying than what I had previously been doing. Change had come in and torn down the invisible fence that had held me back.

Some companies will almost desperately cling to anything that seems to work. As a speaker at corporate meetings, I have often seen the first reaction to something on the agenda that works to be, "Be sure we do that again next year! Everyone liked it!" If they loved my speech then they want to book me for next year. What they should do is say, "Okay. Calloway was good. Now let's go the other way and find somebody completely different with an opposite point of view and see what kind of thought that will provoke." There's a point of diminishing returns that is reached very·quickly today with almost anything that works. Don't think: "It worked. Do it again." Think: "It worked. Now what will work next?"

The strategy of sticking with what works would be fine if only the marketplace and the rest of the world would say, "Okay. We'll stop, too." But customers never stop wanting more, new, and better. Technology doesn't take a break. Society doesn't ever settle down and reach agreement on what the rules are. Everything moves forward all the time and if the rate of change outside your company ever exceeds the rate of change inside your company, you've got trouble.

From Resisting to Running

Category of One companies learn to create their own sense of urgency without waiting for a crisis to come down the road and shake them out of complacency. Consistently successful companies often take the view that they are never more than a few years away from complete and total failure, and they must be constantly taking steps to avoid that failure. Others take the approach that they are always in the process of making what they do obsolete, looking ahead five or six years to see where their industry and their customers are going to be in order to waiting for them when they arrive. Far from resisting change, they are running with change to create their own future rather than leave it to chance and circumstances out of their control.

There is a cycle of success that demands an ongoing process of innovation and change. Whatever you are doing that works will run its course with a period of initial introduction to the marketplace, then, hopefully, followed by a peak of popularity, with a period of inevitable decline coming after. What you have to do is to introduce the next thing while what you are doing is at its peak of popularity, so that you continually replace what is declining with what is ascending.

What about products that seem to stay around forever, unchanged? It's true that the product may stay the same, but the marketing of the product will have to go through the cycle of success to keep pace with changes in how people make buying decisions. People might buy a soft drink because it's perceived as being a good energy boost during the day, then it becomes a product preferred because of taste, then because it's perceived as being cool, then because it's endorsed by popular cultural or sports figures. The product may not change, but the reasons people buy the product will change. Nothing stays the same.

Success Creates a New Reality

The very act of becoming successful demands that you change. The classic example would be the person in a corporate organization that rises to the level of their incompetence. It could be the star salesperson who, because of her tremendous success in sales, is promoted to sales manager. Now she has to learn a whole new set of skills to survive, much less continue to succeed.

In the early days of my career as a speaker on business, I was fortunate enough to receive rave reviews almost every time I gave a speech. I was often told that I was the best speaker the group had ever heard. With that success came a corresponding change in my fees (they went up!) as well as a change in my clients. I moved from speaking to relatively small companies with limited budgets to working with larger companies with big budgets. As I moved up this ladder of success, the reality of my marketplace changed.

Not only did the standards of performance get tougher but the expectations of the clients went up. And my competitors who were moving up the ladder with me were very, very good. They had also had that same experience of being "the best speaker we've ever had." So you've got this survival-of-the-fittest dynamic happening that continued to change the playing field and demanded that I make changes in my work. I was forced to get better or go back down the ladder.

Luckily, I thrive on that kind of competition and find that it's much more rewarding for me personally to make significant changes on a continuing basis, rather than assume that what got me here will keep me here. It won't. Whatever you've done to get successful, it won't be enough to keep you successful. You have to move on to the next thing or be prepared to lose ground. There's very little maintaining of your position these days. You're either moving forward or backward. It's like running a race in which you have to go out and reach your maximum speed as quickly as possible, and then increase your speed on each subsequent lap. You have to take things up a notch or you're going to go backward.

I Don't Know

It may sound like a frantic and stressful way to do business but the opposite is actually true. The goal is to be like a duck. Above the surface, the duck appears to be gliding across the pond smoothly and gracefully, while under the surface he's paddling like hell. The Category of One companies where continuous change is the norm are those very companies that appear to be gliding across the pond of business smoothly and gracefully. There may be a level of chaos going on, but it's a welcomed and managed chaos.

So what's the secret? What's the key to changing effectively? I believe that the key can be found in the concept of not knowing. The individuals and companies that I have worked with who excel at change are those who accept the idea that they don't know what's going to happen next, and are perfectly okay with not knowing. That doesn't mean that they are frozen into inaction. It means that they can navigate periods of uncertainty with the confidence that whatever happens, they can make the appropriate adjustments and will handle it in a way that creates opportunity.

When I go into a convention to give a keynote speech, I always have a general outline prepared based on my research and understanding of the company and the industry. As the meeting moves through its agenda, however, I listen to the company's internal speakers and gauge the interest and mood of the audience, all the while making changes in my presentation. By the time I take the stage to give my speech, my notes are almost always a seemingly undecipherable mess of scribbled notes, marked out paragraphs, and arrows that connect points in a truly mysterious pattern. You might think that my competitive strength would come from always knowing exactly what I'm going to say in my speeches. On the contrary, my strength comes from never knowing what I'm going to say, because I don't know what's going to happen at that meeting until I get there.

Whatever Happens Is Normal

One of the most valuable ideas I've ever discovered in terms of creating calm in the midst of a storm, and helping me keep my head when those about me are losing theirs, is the idea that whatever happens is normal. Not that whatever happens is always desirable or even acceptable, but that it's almost always normal. A simple example of that would be having a flight canceled because of bad weather. Now this might wreck your schedule and cause you to have to completely rethink your plans, but, as a very, very frequent flyer, let me assure you that canceled flights are normal indeed.

Because I see canceled flights as normal, I don't go into a tailspin when it happens. I know what to do to either create an alternate way of getting there or, at the very least, minimize the damage that may come from not getting where I wanted to be at the anticipated time. All around me I see people, some of whom are obviously seasoned travelers, going into complete states of panic and anger over what is really a very common occurrence. I wonder if they just haven't been paying attention for the past 20 years or what.

This idea that "whatever happens is normal" is what separates those who handle change effectively from those who go ballistic at the slightest deviation from what they had expected. We've all seen both types. On the one hand is the person who, if you tell them that there's been a change in plans, policy, schedule, the menu, or virtually anything else, will quite completely lose it. They will either sink into a fuming funk or launch into a scream rant. Either way, they don't do well when the plans change.

The other end of the spectrum is that person who, regardless of what kind of changes you throw at them, seems to handle it almost effortlessly. This person tends to be among the most valuable in an organization. The value of a person with the ability to perform well under pressure cannot be overestimated in a world where constant pressure is the norm.

It Depends on How You Look at It

Some companies have a knack for creating opportunity out of virtually any set of economic or market conditions. Certainly Category of One companies, as well as individuals, have the ability to make lemonade out of lemons. I don't believe that this ability comes from any particular motivational hocus pocus, but instead from a quite simple truth: it depends on how you look at it. Perception is reality. Certainly I can say that my perception is my reality and your perception is your reality. The challenge is to choose a perception that is most likely to create opportunity.

This isn't a case of wishful thinking or sugarcoating difficult situations. It's really a matter of being creative enough and tough enough to create an opportunity when your competition can't. Creative perception is the ability to look at the same thing as everyone else and see something different. When faced with a difficult problem or unexpected change that, at first look, seems to be trouble, I have learned to always remind myself that there is another way of looking at it.

For companies that have mastered this art and skill of creative perception, what are difficult times for others prove to be opportunities for them. I was in the real estate business in the late 1970s when the interest rate skyrocketed almost overnight. This sudden spike in the interest rate came after a few years during which selling real estate was like bobbing for water. You couldn't miss. When rates went up, many of our competitors waved the white flag and a number of them got out of the business altogether.

My approach to a tight market has always been that it's the best time to capture market share. When things are easy, anybody can do it. Companies that are truly good at what they do welcome occasional tough times, because it invites their competition to find another line of work. This isn't any kind of motivational positive thinking at work. To me, it's just business. Why would I choose to look at it in any other way? How would that make me any money?

The Lesson of White Water

One of my favorite outdoor activities is white-water rafting. It's a great way to experience nature while at the same time really challenging yourself in many ways.

The greatest lesson I ever learned about getting a team through change and the unknown was on a white-water rafting trip on the Middle Fork of the Salmon River. It was a fabulous trip. One week shooting the rapids and enjoying some of the most beautiful scenery in the world with about a dozen other people in our group. Our river guide and leader was a tall, skinny redheaded fellow who was soft-spoken and who chose his words very carefully. He was one of those leaders who didn't waste his words on mindless chatter. When he did say something, it was generally something of significance that was well worth listening to.

On the third day of the trip, we approached a series of rapids that looked almost out of control. The water level of the river was such that these normally difficult rapids had gone to the next level. They were thunderous. They were intimidating. They were flat out scary.

The other river raft expeditions in front of us had all pulled up onto the river bank and the leaders of each were standing alongside the rapids, trying to figure out the best way to get through this mass of churning, foaming, wild water. I tagged along with our river guide as he joined his colleagues on the bank to survey the situation. "Take a look at this," one of the other guides said, pointing wide-eyed at the rapids. Our guide took one look and quietly said, "Wow. Now that'll get your attention." After standing and looking and thinking for a few moments, he said, "Okay. Let's go." Then he turned on his heels and strode purposefully back toward our rafts. "Wait a minute," one of the other guides said. "You telling us you've got a plan?" "Nah." our guide replied. "We'll make it up while we're screaming."

Every Paddle in the Water

When our guide got back to the group, he explained very calmly and very clearly the potential dangers of going through this particular set of rapids. "It's not everybody's cup of tea to go through this kind of water," he said. "And if you're not up for it, that's fine. Sometimes I'm not either."

"But if you do go along, I need you to look me and all of your fellow rafters in the eye and make an absolute gut level commitment that you're in all the way. It is absolutely essential," he said, "that I have *every paddle in the water*. It's the only way we'll make it through and have this thing be a ton of fun and not a very wet, very cold swim for all of us."

It's been said that the most important decision an organization can make isn't what to do, but who's going to do it. That means that before you charge headfirst into the changes necessary to take it to the next level, you'd better decide if everyone on the train is really on board with their entire heart and soul.

Our guide then proceeded to have a little one-on-one chat with each of us, in which he asked about our willingness to go and our commitment to have our paddles in the water. He also looked each one of us right in the eyes and did some soul-searching on his own to go beyond what each of us was saying and get a feel for what was really in our heart of hearts. He had to be sure of our commitment to the decision.

A critically important point that our guide made with us was about the need for immediate response. He said, "This is what we call on the river a learning opportunity. Normally when we go through a rapid, you know that I tell you in advance what line we're going to take and what our strategy will be. On this rapid," he said, "all I can tell you right now is that we're going in on the left side. Beyond that, and it's very important that you understand this, I will give you information as it becomes available to me. If I say paddle left, then by gosh you'd better paddle left with everything you've got and without hesitation. Stay focused," he said, "and we'll be fine. We'll do what we need to do when we need to do it."

A few members of the group decided to walk around and not take the raft through the rapids. That was fine and everyone appreciated their honesty. For those of us who did sign on to take the ride, we were very focused on what we were undertaking, totally committed to the task, and ready to handle whatever the river threw at us. The story has a gloriously happy ending, as we were able to successfully negotiate the rapids in what was the most fun I've ever had on a river.

There were a handful of lessons that came from that experience, all of which have served me well in business. We got the right people on board, the ones who were committed. We had every paddle in the water. We responded to changes with purpose, intention, and confidence. It's no different for a company that is facing the white water of change, whether external or internal change.

As Quill undertook its white-water journey to take the company to the next level, these same principals came into play. Larry Morse of Quill put it this way, "It is crucial that as many people be on board as possible. Going to the next level requires constant focus and attention. It requires teams to do the things that other teams won't do in other companies to get to the next level. We continuously look at ways to reinvent our service and add additional services that our competitors do not have. It takes a very conscious decision to go for it and we have to remind ourselves of this every day."

Bobby Bradley of CST agrees, "Everybody's got to be on board. They just have to be. If they're not, you have to figure out why they're not and fix it. If they're not getting on board even though we're trying to work with them and fix it—then they have to go. We can't assume everyone is on board. People revert back to basic behavior patterns and may not be in line with vision. We have to do whatever it takes to keep them on board. Managers have to be the example. They have to recognize people living the brand—and reinforce it."

The Hard Truth

As tough and as painful as it is to deal with, sometimes the bottom line hard truth is that people can end up playing on a team that really isn't any longer a good match for them. It's as wrong for the individual as it is for the organization. Once either party realizes that it's a square peg in a round hole situation, then the best thing for both parties is to deal with that reality honestly and supportively and work together to find a solution. Sometimes that solution is that someone leaves and finds another place to work.

It's like joining a team in the basketball league down at the local gym where you work out, thinking that this will be a pleasant way to spend Saturday mornings and get some good exercise through a fun activity. You can also meet some people and perhaps create some new friendships.

Then you discover that you've gotten into something way beyond what you bargained for. These people are serious. They're on a take-no-prisoners mission in what turns out to be, for your teammates, a life or death quest to win the basketball league championship. They expect you to attend three practices a week, devote yourself to a strict fitness regimen, and make this team the center of your existence. You decide that you don't want to play anymore because it's not fun for you.

That's perfectly okay! Just because it's fun for the others does not mean that it's going to be fun for you. Find another place to play. You'll be happier, they'll be happier, and no one will resent your decision. It's the same sometimes in business. Sometimes people need to move to another team in another league. There's no right or wrong involved. It's not a matter of moral superiority of any kind. It's a matter of different strokes for different folks.

The Most Fun and the Most Afraid

It's constant white water. Sometimes change is at once the most fun you'll ever have and the most afraid you'll ever be. Category of One companies love the challenge, and they always know that it's more fun going through the rapids than it is standing on the riverbank. Standing to the side on the riverbank may seem like a safe place to be, but if you don't develop the will and the skills to get through the white water, you'll be stuck there forever.

The Commodity Trap

Done While You Wait

About 10 miles south of Louisville, Kentucky, on Interstate 65, there is what I consider to be the greatest billboard in the world. It's a billboard that is obviously meant to entertain as well as advertise, and its message was composed with someone's tongue placed firmly in cheek. There are no photographs or pictures, only six wonderful words spelled out in giant, garish, day-glo colored letters. It says, simply:

Tattoo Charley's
Done While You Wait

The billboard barely registered in my mind until about five miles farther along the road when I suddenly thought, "Well,

74

of course, it's done while you wait! It's a TATTOO parlor! It has to be done while you wait! ALL tattoo parlors do it while you wait!" And that, of course, is the joke that Tattoo Charlie is sharing with the world. He's saying "Do business with us because we do exactly the same thing as our competition."

Sad but True

The most basic competitive question is this: "Why should I do business with you?" Most companies answer that most competitive question in a most noncompetitive way. The sad truth of the matter is that most companies go to the market with pretty much the same message as Tattoo Charley. The difference is that Tattoo Charley means it as a joke. Everyone else is serious. What they're doing, without realizing it, is saying to the world "Do business with us, because we're pretty much the same as our competition, but we're really good at it." Not much differentiation there.

The marketplace has become "commoditized." Customers see parity everywhere. They look at you or me or any other business out there and they believe that they can get pretty much the same thing, just as good, for a similar or lower price, from the competition. And the fact is that they're exactly right. We are all commodities. We're all like a pound of nails. There's no difference in any of us except for price. No difference, that is, until we do something to change the customer's perception of us.

Transcending Commodity

The great challenge for any business today is to transcend commodity. If customers see you as offering basically the same product and service as your competitors, the only way you can compete is with price. So either you choose to play the "we're the cheapest," low margin, lowest price game, or you change the game. To avoid the price war trap, you must change the customer's basis of comparison. You must, in fact, transcend commodity and, if you're really good, defy comparison.

We've all heard the old saying that someone is trying to "compare apples and oranges." Well that's exactly what you want to create with your business. You want to be an apple and have all of your competitors be seen as oranges. You transcend commodity by creating a difference with customers through their experience of what it's *like* to do business with you. It's very rarely done with product or technology alone. It's almost always most effectively done with people. The price of entry into the game of business today is that you must have a quality product and offer good service at a competitive price. That's just the beginning. Then the *real* competition starts.

The Starting Point

The first step in transcending commodity is to recognize that the marketplace sees you as a commodity. That's your starting point. Don't fight that idea. Go with it. It's a competitively powerful perspective to say, "You know, we really are pretty much the same as our competitors. Now, what are we going to do about that?"

This is not about putting yourself down. It's about getting realistic and seeing your company through the eyes of your customers and potential customers. It's been said that to catch a fish, think like a fish, not a fisherman. Consider this an exercise in thinking like a fish.

The Trap of the False Promise

One of the most treacherous aspects of the commodity trap is that many companies, in their efforts to not be seen as a commodity, try to differentiate themselves with false promises. It's a simple strategy: "Let's make up things to tell people that will convince them we're better than our competition. Let's just lay claim to superiority. After all, who's going to check?" The first thing that comes to mind for me is that this strategy won't work because it's betting on the stupidity of the customer.

You have to wonder what would possess anyone in his right mind, or even half a right mind, to promise customers more than he even come close to delivering. Are these same people not customers themselves? Have they not experienced the frustration, disgust, and anger that comes from being promised a great customer experience and not getting it? Do they honestly not realize the incredible damage that over-promising does in the eyes of the marketplace? This strategy doesn't differentiate a business, it destroys a business.

Danger Signs

I had gone to San Antonio on a business trip and as I checked into my hotel I was greeted with signs everywhere all proclaiming the hotel's new advertising campaign:

Better Than Our Competition.

This was a major hotel chain and it looked like a national program. There was a big sign in the lobby, a little sign on the registration desk, a button on the desk clerk's lapel, another sign in the elevator, and signs all over my room, all of which said: "*Better* Than Our Competition." As it turned out, these were danger signs.

Imagine my surprise and joy when I also discovered in my room an impressive tray of goodies that had been left there for me by the manager. There was also an explanatory note that explained that I had been named "Customer of the Month." As "Customer of the Month" I got an ice bucket with a few long-neck beers, a party tray with salsa and chips, and a straw cowboy hat. Yee haa! So far, so good.

The manager's note asked me to perform a simple, yet important favor for the hotel. In return for the goodies, I was asked to complete a fairly extensive feedback survey. They claimed to be "*Better* Than Our Competition" in all ways, and wanted to know how I thought they were doing. Fine. Pop open the first longneck and have at it.

Boy, Did They Pick the Wrong Guy

Actually, they picked the right guy, depending on whether or not they used the information I gave them, because the feedback I gave them took the form of a major roasting. I hammered them. I wanted to get their attention and have them realize the incredible folly of this absurd "*Better* Than Our Competition" marketing campaign of theirs.

It was as if some knucklehead in their marketing department said, "Well, we know we're really not better than our competition, and we probably really are a commodity with nothing to distinguish ourselves from anyone else. But to change a lot of things and really get better at what we do would take too much time and effort and money. So let's not get better but let's just *say* we're better which will get us more customers and won't cost anything beyond making up a bunch of signs!"

I'll not bore you with the list of deficiencies in that hotel, but suffice it to say that from the surly front desk clerk to the lack of cleanliness in the room and the burned out light bulbs and . . . well, you get the idea. "*Better* Than Our Competition"???? If they hadn't brought it up it wouldn't have been nearly as noticeable how truly deficient they were. I would have just chalked it up to another night in another thoroughly mediocre hotel. But "*Better* Than Our Competition"!!!! The nerve, the unmitigated GALL of such an obviously bogus claim made my head spin. As I drank more of the free beers, I had to get extra paper for my commentary, which was now approaching novella length.

You Can't Advertise Your Way to Superior Performance

The saddest aspect of the whole debacle was that somewhere, some marketing vice president without a clue was proud as punch for coming up with this exceptionally clever and strikingly original concept: "*Better* Than Our Competition." There's an old saying: Don't wrestle with a pig. You just get dirty and it annoys the pig. Let me add: Don't claim to be something that you are not. You just look stupid and it annoys the customer. It will actually go beyond annoyance. It will probably lose you the customer's business.

You can't just advertise your way to superior performance, and yet it's absolutely amazing how many companies try to do just that. They have ideas like "Hey! Let's do an advertising campaign! Let's tell everybody our service is great! Let's *not* improve our service and say we did!!!"

I was doing some consulting work with a really big bank that was losing market share. Instead of doing the hard work necessary to improve customer relationships and service, they decided to run an advertising campaign instead! How clever. All the benefits of improved customer service with none of the effort! Their advertising campaign was "People Matter Most."

Guess who saw through the "People Matter Most" ad campaign first. The employees. They doubled over with laughter. They cried real tears and patted their bellies. They squealed. What a stitch! "People Matter Most." Yeah. Right. And donkeys fly and jaybirds wear derby hats. The customers weren't falling for it either. In fact, the bank ended up with a much worse problem than they had started with. Their goofy, false promise-based ad campaign called attention to what, in fact, was their greatest weakness. They were terrible at dealing with people.

Customers Know the Truth

The fact is, you can't fool very many people much of the time at all. If you want to run an advertising campaign that tells the world how great you are, here's a little tip.

Get great first because the customers know the truth. They always know. What businesses used to get away with in terms of false promises simply won't work anymore. Today's customer is flexing her newly discovered economic muscles. And she won't be lied to. Yesterday's sense of helplessness has been replaced with a new determination, almost a militancy that won't allow deception.

Not only will today's customers leave if they feel mislead or mistreated, they'll look for justice. That justice is likely to take the form of letters to the Better Business Bureau, calls to the consumer advocate at the local television news bureau, or even hiring an attorney to pursue legal action. All for what used to be considered just the "normal" exaggeration of claims for a product or service. Today we must deliver what we promise, or more. If you say you can do it, you'd darn well better do it. Don't make promises you can't keep.

Beyond Expected Factors

To avoid the commodity trap you have to find points of genuine differentiation. For most companies, that will mean looking in places they've neglected up to now. It will mean going beyond the expected factors of price, quality, and service.

Occasionally, I'll talk with someone who tells me that in his or her type of business, it's all about price. They will say that their buyers look strictly for the lowest price and that there's nothing else that will really influence them. If that is really true, then you quite literally only have two choices. You have to figure out a way to have the lowest price and still make a profit or the game is over for you.

If, in fact, the business you're in is all about price, either figure out how to have the lowest price and still make a profit or find something else to do. However, what's more likely true is that you're just taking the easy way out and blaming your failure to differentiate on your mistaken belief that your customers only consider price, which is seldom reality. Buyers of anything are looking for value. They are looking for a way to solve problems or create opportunities. No matter what the buyer says, price is never the only consideration. Value always has and always will be the primary buying factor.

Beyond Price and Product

But what if you truly are selling a commodity? What if your product really is a pound of nails? Isn't price the only way you can compete? Well, let's look at the companies that sell pounds of nails and see what's going on in that marketplace.

Home Depot, Lowe's, True Value Hardware, and other hardware and building supplies retailers all sell pretty much the same products. These are companies that really *do* sell pounds of nails. And they all advertise low prices. If the game ended there, then lowest price would always win.

In the hardware and building supply business, however, what's happened is that because they *are* selling what many people consider commodities, they have to offer something more than just low price to keep customers happy. In this business, the name of the game has become who can do the best job of helping you use the product. It's gone far beyond price to the areas of solving problems and making your home improvement dreams come true.

Singing on the Plane

When Herb Kelleher started Southwest Airlines, he knew he was entering a commodity business. At its simplest level, the airline business is a matter of putting people in seats and getting them from point A to point B. That's pretty much a commodity.

Southwest decided to be a low price competitor, and it's a foundation of their business, but low price alone isn't enough.

Other low fare carriers provide price competition for Southwest, as well as the major airlines that will match Southwest's fares on many routes.

At Southwest they've done a great job of competing at the commodity level. They have low prices, run the business with tremendous efficiency, and give good service. The true differentiation, however, comes in their ability to make the traveling experience a fun one. Anyone who has taken more than a handful of Southwest flights knows that their employees take a totally different approach to flying. They have been charged by the company to make flying fun, and so you'll see ticket agents in costume at Halloween, hear gate agents making jokes with waiting passengers as they board the flight, and experience songs, games, and otherwise outrageous behavior by the flight attendants on the plane. All in the interests of avoiding the commodity trap.

These Southwest Airlines stories are warm and fuzzy, but does their approach to avoiding the commodity trap really work? According to the U.S. Department of Transportation, Southwest regularly scores higher in customer satisfaction and performance measures than any of its competitors. The company consistently ranks in the Top Ten of *Fortune*'s "Most Admired Companies." And in one of the toughest businesses in the world, Southwest has been consistently profitable for over three decades.

It's Just Easier

The battle to win customers in the retail grocery business is one that has long been fought with price. Running specials, offering discount coupons, and giving lower prices with a membership card remain key elements in grocery store competition.

But more and more grocers are realizing that they have to find something beyond that low price expectation to win and keep customers.

H.G. Hill Food Stores is a regional grocery chain that has discovered that, in addition to the low prices that customers expect, the way for them to escape the commodity trap is through creating value in the customer's shopping experience. A recent H.G. Hill ad campaign featured the claim that they have more cashiers on duty and will get you out of the store quicker than their competitors. The ads centered around the promise that "It's just easier at H.G. Hill's." This goes beyond what the customer expects, which is a good product at a competitive price. This gets to the idea of "what it's like" to do business with you.

The real competitive battle is being fought beyond traditional notions of service in areas such as who can best solve your problem, who can offer you the most help in using the product, or what experience or feeling is created for the customer. Even in the selling of true commodities, like hammers and nails, seats on airplanes, or groceries, it's never a matter of just price and product.

Way beyond Quality

Think about where you differentiate. Or, more accurately, where you don't. It's probably not with your product. Oh sure, we all take pride in whatever product we make or sell. We believe in the quality of our product. But the truth is that the quality playing field got leveled a long time ago. It's rare that anyone gains a competitive edge strictly through product quality anymore.

Consider what you might think is the opposite end of the spectrum from being a commodity. Let's look at the business of selling luxury cars. BMW is one of the many car companies I've worked with over the years. BMW is a company that is obsessed with quality, and it shows in the craftsmanship of their product. BMW is also a relatively expensive car.

Years ago, BMW's quality alone was enough to merit a high price. If someone questioned the value of a BMW, the response could pretty well be summed up in one word: quality. And the quality was there. You pay for what you get and in a BMW you were getting a truly fine automobile with an impressive warranty and a reputation for performance and dependability.

Consider two important factors in today's automotive marketplace. Everyone makes a good car today. Everyone. While just a few years ago, quality was truly a differentiator and there was a clear difference between the well-made cars like BMW, Nissan, Mercedes, and Toyota and the not-so-well-made cars like almost everyone else, that quality gap has now disappeared. Look at the warranty on a car like Hyundai. It's impressive, to say the least, and as good a warranty as is offered by many cars costing thousands more.

The other factor to consider is the question of who you are being compared to. Who is BMW compared to? Mercedes, Lexus, Jaguar, Audi, Cadillac, and other top automobiles are who you compare BMW to. So we're right back to comparing quality with quality. We're back to being a pound of nails. BMW is a commodity just like all other high-performance luxury cars when they are compared to their peers.

But many car companies, certainly the ones that will succeed now and in the future, are like BMW in that they know that quality is an entry-level factor, not really a differentiator anymore. BMW is still obsessed with quality, and I believe they always will be. But BMW is also working very hard, as are many of their competitors, to create a compelling ownership experience that will insure customer loyalty. The irony is that when you create a truly high quality product, you compete only against the other high quality products, so the competitive battle shifts away from quality to other areas.

It's Your People?

Tell me something your competition can't. Differentiate for me. Come on. I dare you. Why should I do business with you instead of the company down the street that does the same thing? What do you do different? I know what you're going to say. You're going to pull out that triple top-secret weapon that you think is the ultimate differentiator in the battle for customers. You're going to say, "It's our people! We've got great people who are great at what they do and really care about the customer."

Wow. I'm just impressed beyond words. And you know, you're right. That's the big difference. That's what sets you apart from your competition. Because I asked your competitor the same thing, and she had to admit that her people:

- Are terrible at what they do,
- Have no training,
- Know nothing about their products,
- Tend to be boorish and rude,
- Treat the customers like dirt!

Let's get real. If your competition had incompetent bullies working for them, they'd all be out of business, you'd be rich, and you'd rule the marketplace.

So your people are better? Prove it. What do they do that your competition doesn't do? How is your training better? What do your people do with customers that blows the competition away? Prove it. Because if you *can* prove it, you've got something incredible. People, in fact, can be that great differentiator that enables you to transcend commodity and defy comparison.

Your Competition Already Said It

A few years ago, I was doing an extensive sales training program with the branch managers of a big bank. One of the exercises that I had them do was to simulate a sales presentation. The scenario I presented them was this: They were going to be giving a presentation to a potential customer who had already heard sales presentations by all of their competitors. They were to come up with things that would clearly differentiate their bank from the other banks. I instructed them to not talk about such entry-level factors as having a complete line of accounts and services, or having convenient locations, or about having good, well-trained people. Any of their competitors could say the same thing and it would be the truth. The assignment was to differentiate by going beyond expected factors.

The next day, my eager bankers began to give their presentations. And one after another, over and over, they said the same things:

"We would encourage you to do business with our banks because we offer a complete line of accounts and services."

"We have a number of conveniently located branches."

"We feel that our greatest advantage is our people! You will find that all of our employees are friendly and well trained to serve your needs."

It was like some weird banking episode of The Bank Twilight Zone. Or The Stepford Bankers. They were so stuck in their same old approaches that they just couldn't break free. It was like listening to preprogrammed zombies who had been taught that what all good, proper bankers must say to compete politely and without any pesky thinking involved was simply "it's our people." They just couldn't process the idea that their competitors also had good, friendly, happy, shiny people. We spent the rest of the sales training working on creative ways to differentiate the people here from the people at their competitors. And they discovered that to truly be able to make the claim "We're better. It's our people!" that they would have to create a real advantage in their people.

What do you know that your competition doesn't know? Do you have a skill that they don't have? Do you know more about customers and their needs than your competitors do? Maybe the difference in your people can be found in attitude. Taking personal responsibility, for instance.

Superstar

I remember when I moved my offices and made arrangements to get telephone service installed. I made an appointment for the phone company installer to be at our offices at 8:00 A.M. on Monday morning. 8:00 A.M. came and went—no installer.

At 9:00 A.M., I called (from a cell phone) and was told that the appointment was scheduled, but they didn't know what had happened or why the installer hadn't shown up. At 10:00 A.M. I called and never could even get connected with the right department. At 11:00 A.M. I called and was told that I'd have to find out the number of the installation department and call them directly. I'm not the brightest guy in the world, but I could see a definite pattern developing here.

My final call, in desperation, was to the general number of the phone company. I asked to be connected with the installation department. After a few moments on hold, a young man cheerfully answered, "Accounts Payable, may I help you?" I took a deep breath, and, as calmly as was humanly possible, asked the young man to try and connect me with installation. He astutely detected that there was some sort of problem and asked me to explain the situation. I gave him a brief rundown of the problem and said that I knew it wasn't his problem and that I wasn't his customer and I asked again to be connected to installation.

The young man said, "Sir, you've got me on the phone. That means you're my customer now and it's my problem now. I'm going to give you my name and extension number. If an installer isn't at your office within 30 minutes, I want you to call back and ask for me personally. I'm going to take care of this, sir. Don't worry about it another minute."

Now, that's what it means when you say, "Our people make the difference." Just one problem, though. This was one person out of the five or six I had dealt with that morning who was willing to take responsibility. So this particular company would have been able to say, at best, "ONE of our people makes a difference." And that's not nearly good enough.

Companies sometimes are so proud of their "superstar" performers that they forget this simple truth—superstars don't win games. Teams win games. Michael Jordan was basketball's ultimate superstar, but without Scotty Pippin and the rest of the Chicago Bulls he might never have won championships. I'll trade in all of my superstars for a team of steady, consistent performers any day.

When People Truly Are the Differentiator

If, in fact, your people really ARE the difference, and you can say that about ALL of them, then you have a powerful advantage, indeed. So the challenge becomes to create that advantage and then be able to prove it. While creating an advantage with people is your best shot at creating a Category of One company, transcending commodity, and defying comparison, it's not an easy thing to achieve.

After all, you're dealing with people. They're all different in a thousand ways—different talents, attitudes, motivations, hopes, dreams, and aspirations. The trick is to create a consistency of performance and "feeling" while not creating clones. Customers have a very accurate built-in "BS" detector that can see through fake or forced behavior from a mile away.

I often ask my audiences to tell me about a business that has completely won their loyalty as a customer. It's a real world survey of the marketplace talking about what it takes to win and keep customers. What's amazing is that no matter what type of business is discussed, there always seems to be a common thread that runs through all of these great companies. The challenge for you is to think about what these companies do and ask yourself if your company does the same thing. If not, why not? And don't let the fact that the company is in a completely different kind of business stop you. You have to be creative enough to figure out what *your version* would look like, and then take it and make it work for you.

Here's a classic example of what most people would consider a commodity business that has used people to transcend commodity, and win customers for life. Whenever I work in the northwestern United States, I hear many people mention a very unique tire company, Les Schwab Tires. What strikes me as particularly significant about Les Schwab Tires is the level of consistency of performance that they've been able to achieve in the area of customer relations and service.

They Run to the Car

One of my favorite things to do when working with a business audience is to demonstrate how a company, through sheer creativity and consistency of performance with its people, can differentiate itself to the point that it truly creates a Category of One in its market area. If I am working with a group comprised of people from all over the United States, I'll ask the people from the Pacific Northwest to identify themselves by raising their hands. I then say that in their part of the country there is a company that is a truly extraordinary example of transcending commodity because of the performance of its people. At this point, I sometimes have someone correctly guess the company I'm thinking of. If no one does, all I have to do is say, "They sell tires."

Immediately I will get a response from almost everyone who is from the Pacific Northwest, in unison, "Les Schwab!" Then I turn to the entire audience and tell them to think about the significance of what just happened. All I did was say that in this part of the country there is an extraordinary company that sells tires, and everyone named the same company. That is truly a Category of One. There are dozens, maybe hundreds of tire companies large and small, national chains, and mom and pop corner stores, that could have been named. But they always name the same one, Les Schwab Tires. Why?

Les Schwab Tires is one of the largest independent tire dealers in the United States. The Les Schwab Tires customers in my audiences all seem to agree that on the entry-level commodity factors, Les Schwab does a good job. They offer good quality tires at a competitive price, carry a huge inventory offering a great selection, offer an excellent written warranty on the tires, and give good service. But what really differentiates Les Schwab Tires is what they do beyond price, product quality, and even what most people would normally define as service.

I will ask my Pacific Northwesterners how many of them are customers of Les Schwab Tires. A good number of them always are. I will then ask those Les Schwab Tires customers to shout out to the rest of the group what happens when you drive your car into a Les Schwab parking lot. They all shout together "They run to the car!"

That's it. They run to the car. You can be sure that running to the car doesn't happen by accident. Les Schwab Tires calls it "sudden service."

So what's the big deal about running to the car? Just this. With the simple act of running to the car, Les Schwab Tires sends a powerful message to every customer. It is a message that says, "We want and appreciate your business." It is pure genius. It differentiates them to the point that when I ask for people to name an extraordinary company that sells tires only one name comes up: Les Schwab Tires.

In my keynote speech for the Produce Marketing Association Annual Meeting in Philadelphia, Pennsylvania, in 2001 we did the Les Schwab exercise, and, as usual, it worked like a charm. There were many Les Schwab Tires customers there and they testified to the effectiveness of "running to the car." After the speech, a man from Fresno, California, approached me with his own Les Schwab Tires story.

He said that on a vacation trip to Bend, Oregon, he noticed that all four of his tires were in pretty bad shape. He spotted a Lew Schwab Tires store and, even though unfamiliar with them, pulled in to buy a new set of tires. He was greeted by an employee running to his car, and was ultimately very satisfied with the price, product, and service he received. What really impressed him, though, was what happened after he returned to Fresno.

He said that after a couple of weeks something caused one of the tires to go flat. He had gotten the written warranty with the tires, so he called the Les Schwab Tires store in Bend, where a helpful employee pulled up the record of his transaction on the computer. The employee told him not to worry, that they would ship a new replacement tire overnight, at no cost to him, and for him to have the tire installed at the local tire store of his choice in Fresno, then send Les Schwab Tires the bill and they would reimburse him.

How do you transcend commodity? You do it by making good on all those things that most companies claim to do but seldom come through on. When you say that you "exceed your customers' expectations" it means that it doesn't matter what it takes or what it costs to do it, you just do it. When you say that "our people make the difference" then there truly is something extraordinary that your people do that makes people say "Wow. No one else does that!" You go beyond price, product, and service to create a separate category in the minds of customers. You create a Category of One.

What's Your Version?

Now the challenge is yours. Even though the chances are that your business is very different than the retail tire business, what's your *version* of running to the car? For me, as a business consultant and speaker, running to the car might be when a prospective client tells me that she would want me to have a good understanding of her company and industry. I might then offer to spend a day in their headquarters, at no charge, so that I can have a good grasp of who they are and what they want to accomplish. Better yet, in my initial conversation with a prospect, I have already researched the company to the point that I demonstrate an impressive understanding of them and their business. That's running to the car.

A few years ago my wife needed braces and our dentist referred her to an orthodontist with a great reputation, Dr. Joel Gluck. Everything at the commodity level was excellent. He did a great job, the price was competitive, and his entire staff was warm, caring, and attentive. But what can you do beyond be competent and caring to differentiate if you're an orthodontist? They send flowers. Beautiful flowers. Truly gorgeous flowers. And they call you at home just to be sure you're doing okay with the new braces and see if there's anything they can do. They do their version of running to the car.

Do you? Do you send your customers flowers? Do you call them to see if they're doing okay? Or is that just not done in your business? It usually isn't done by an orthodontist either, but Dr. Gluck and his staff do it anyway.

It's funny, isn't it? People want to know what they can do to be innovative, to transcend commodity, and to differentiate from their competition. But my experience has been that when you suggest something to them that might just do the trick, they too often say, "But that's not done in this business." And that's why you're a commodity. While you explain to me why you just don't send flowers to customers in your business, one of your competitors is probably sending flowers, or the creative equivalent of it, to one of your customers.

Notice Me and I'm Yours

There was an article in a popular women's magazine about "How to Get a Man to Notice You at a Party." The whole premise was that if you spot a guy you're interested in, here are the 10 things you can do to try and get his attention. A woman told her husband about the article and he said it was the stupidest thing he'd ever heard.

"If you want to get a guy to notice you at a party just look at him. Make eye contact for about two seconds and he'll notice you. It's a no-brainer," he said.

Today's customer, whether she's buying a cup of coffee or a fleet of airplanes, is saying, "Pay attention to me." When the audiences I work with do the "my favorite business and why" exercise, this comes out again and again. Pay attention to the customer and you will win them and keep them.

It's the way all kinds of companies avoid the commodity trap. Ritz Carlton customers tell me that what impresses them most isn't the magnificence of the lobbies or the incredibly furnished rooms or the food or even the service. What impresses them most is that when they walk through the hotel, the employees acknowledge them. They say hello and even, when appropriate, initiate pleasant conversations just to be sure everything is okay and that the guest is happy.

The things that win customers' hearts at Disney World are the little things that are done purely with the power of people. When you're riding on one of the trains through the property and the guys doing landscaping work stop and wave, that's Disney's version of running to the car. When my friend Chris Rogers lost his sunglasses on the Space Mountain ride and called the lost and found department, who had found his sunglasses and were holding them for him, that's Disney's version of running to the car. The old clichés begin to ring true: It really *isn't* rocket science. More often than not what wins customers' loyalty and helps a company become a Category of One is that, in addition to doing all of the entry-level commodity things right, they have learned to simply pay attention to their customers.

Your Brand
Is Everything

Your Brand Is in the Customer's Mind

Your brand is not your advertising. Your brand is not your logo. Your brand is not your company name. Your brand is not your product. Your brand may not be at all what you think it is. Your brand may not be what you intend for it to be. You do not own your brand.

Your brand is owned by your customers and anyone else who has an impression of your company. Your brand resides in the minds of your customers, not in your newspaper ads. Your brand is whoever customers think you are, whatever they think is your promise to them, and whether or not they believe that you keep that promise.

Nothing is more important than your brand, because it's what defines you in the marketplace. It should be the top priority of every employee, from the president of the company to the employees in the warehouse to the receptionist, to build, protect, and represent your brand to the best of their ability. If your idea of who you are, what you promise the marketplace, and whether or not you keep that promise matches up with the market's perception of those same factors, then you have a strong brand. A strong brand is what makes you a Category of One company. Your brand is everything.

Do They Love You—Or Just Know Who You Are?

Never forget that it is your customers who decide what your brand really is. If your idea of the brand is different than their idea of the brand, theirs is the only idea that counts. At the end of the day, they are the ones who get to vote, not you. It's as simple as the basic truth that no matter how well you think you're doing, all that counts is how well the customers think you're doing. You can run ads all day long about what a great company you have, but if the customers don't experience that and don't believe it, your brand is a loser.

Never confuse name recognition with brand strength. Exxon had incredible name recognition after the Valdez oil spill. In 2002, Enron had greater name recognition than ever before in its history but it was notoriety because of scandal, not because of brand strength. People may stay away from your products in droves because of your brand. What you want is brand strength, not just brand recognition.

You want customers to love you, not just know who you are. You literally have as many brands as you have customers and people who have an impression of you. If those impressions are bad, then your brand is weak. Consider all the brands that you may have created without even knowing it:

- You transfer a customer four times to different departments and she never has her problem solved. That's your brand.
- You charge a customer extra for something they thought was included in the original price. That's your brand.
- You replace a defective product but no one apologizes to the customer for his trouble. That's your brand.
- You put a telephone customer on hold for over a minute. That's your brand.
- Your Web site is confusing and hard to navigate. That's your brand.
- A repeat customer for many years comes into your store and no one greets her by name. That's your brand.

Most feelings about brands are based on comparison. You may think that your competitors are the other companies that do what you do, but customers don't limit their comparisons like that. All customers may know is that someone else in a business completely different from yours did something great for them that you, in their opinion, were unwilling to do. You may not think it's a fair comparison, but that is the customer's call. Anything that another company does for your customer can have a strong influence on how she rates your brand:

- The other company returns my calls within a couple of hours. You usually take at least 24 hours.
- Everyone at the dry cleaners knows my name. I spend about $30 a week with them. My company spends tens of thousands of dollars every year with you and yet I feel like your employees have no idea who I am.

- My stockbroker calls me to see how I'm doing or if I have any questions about how my stocks are performing. You only call me when you want to sell me something.
- The owner of the service station came out to the self-service gas pump the other day to tell me how much he appreciates my business. No one in your company has ever made that kind of gesture of appreciation to me.

Encounters like these are what make up an individual's impression of a company, which then becomes the company's brand. The lesson that the market teaches is that every single encounter that any customer has with your company is what ultimately makes up your brand.

First by Reputation—Then by Experience

I became very dissatisfied with the health insurance company for my business. The dissatisfaction was because of continuing service problems and annoyances. They were simply difficult to do business with. I fired them. When looking for a replacement company, I made my decision based strictly on brand strength.

I made one phone call to the only company that I was even considering, Blue Cross and Blue Shield of Tennessee. I had no personal experience with them, and really didn't know anyone personally who had recommended them to me. I was going purely on strength of brand, and theirs was, in my estimation, rock solid. Blue Cross and Blue Shield of Tennessee won me as a customer and were reaping the benefits of years of cumulative experiences with customers that had all added up to a solid brand reputation. Their initial brand in my mind was made up of everything they had done up to that point.

From the moment that I became their customer, however, their brand started from scratch. I didn't care and wasn't influenced by reputation anymore. I had little or no interest in their advertising. Once I became a customer, their brand was made up of every single interaction they had with me from that point on. This meant everything from the policy itself and whether or not I found it easy to understand, to the monthly bill and the ease with which we could read it, to the really powerful encounters, which were any that involved dealing with a real person in the company.

If I had a question about an exclusion in the policy, how well did the customer service representative on the phone handle that inquiry? Was she clear and helpful? Was she friendly and professional? How did the physicians I dealt with feel about the company? When I gave my Blue Cross Blue Shield card to someone on the physician's staff, were they happy to see it or did they groan, knowing that it would be a pain to deal with them?

In my case, every experience was positive. The Blue Cross and Blue Shield of Tennessee brand has done nothing but grow in strength based on my experience as a customer.

Get on the Short List

What Blue Cross and Blue Shield of Tennessee had done with their brand power was get on my short list. As a matter of fact, they had created a very, very short list in that they were the only name on it. That's how brand power works for you. It pulls customers right past your competition and into your store, Web site, or catalog.

I recently flew into the Cincinnati airport and was walking to the main terminal to catch a taxi into the city. Before I got a taxi, though, I wanted to buy a particular product. As I made my way through the airport toward the main terminal, I passed a number of establishments selling perfectly good versions of this product. The prices they were asking ranged from about 75 cents to $1.50. There were no lines and I could have easily stopped at any one of them to make the purchase. I walked right past each of them.

When I got to the midpoint of the terminal I was in, I turned away from my destination, the main terminal, and actually went out of my way to go to a particular place that was selling the product I wanted. When I got there, there was a line of about six or seven people. I waited patiently. After a few minutes, I placed my order and cheerfully paid from two to three times more for this product than the other guys were charging.

Can you guess what I bought?

Right. Coffee. Starbucks coffee. That's brand power. I walked past competition that was selling this commodity product for much less in order to buy from a brand that I know, trust, and like. What you want to be and what I want to be is the Starbucks in your particular industry or business.

Laura and Harley

One of the great brand power stories is Harley Davidson. You may think that your business is so different from Harley Davidson's that you have nothing to learn from them. Think again. You can learn lessons from any great brand no matter what business they're in.

I did some work with Witex, a flooring manufacturer based in Atlanta, Georgia. They were doing a series of events around the country for their product rollout of the new line of Laura Ashley Flooring. The idea was to invite their distributor and dealer partners in to learn, not just about Laura Ashley Flooring, but about the power of a strong brand and how it could help their businesses succeed.

Most of the attendees at these events were guys who were unfamiliar with the Laura Ashley brand. But they were all very familiar with Harley Davidson. To help provoke some thinking about brand power, I drew some comparisons between Harley Davidson and Laura Ashley.

Harley Davidson and Laura Ashley are both targeted toward a clearly defined market. The question for the floor distributors and dealers was whether or not Laura Ashley Flooring's target market matched up with their own target market. It just so happens that women between the ages of 25 and 55 are the emerging force as the decision makers in the purchase of home furnishings, so the power of aligning with Laura Ashley became a no-brainer.

Harley Davidson and Laura Ashley are both known for quality products. While Harley had some quality challenges many years ago, they have since very successfully established themselves as a top quality manufacturer. Laura Ashley has an unbroken string of over 50 years as a quality brand.

Both Harley Davidson and Laura Ashley are seen by their customers as being truly one of a kind brands. Nothing sounds like a Harley. Nothing has quite the same style of Laura Ashley.

Both brands are based on the popularity of core products, which help drive the sales of other products. The Harley name is now found on key chains, belts, jackets, posters, radios, and many other products. Laura Ashley started with women's fashions and fabrics and has slowly built the product line. And they've done it in a way that has protected the credibility of the brand.

Perhaps most important, both Harley Davidson and Laura Ashley appeal to customers on an emotional level. That's the magic ingredient. To the extent that your brand can create an emotional connection with your customers, you've created brand strength.

If you think about your own favorite brands, whether it's Wheaties, Disney World, Land's End, or Apple computers, you probably have some level of emotional connection with that brand. Brand strength ultimately goes beyond product. It goes to people.

Doing the Work versus Telling the Story

It's not the job of the marketing, advertising, or public relations departments to create the brand. They have a hand in it, just like everyone else in the company. But their job is to tell the story of the brand. It's the job of everyone else in the company to create the brand with the quality of how they do their work everyday. For years, people defined branding as the process of creating an ad campaign or marketing program that conveyed a desirable image to the public. That's fine as far as it goes and these efforts can certainly help the brand. But it's nothing when compared to the power of how people actually experience your company. That's your brand.

When the advertising doesn't match with the reality, then you've really got a problem. A few years ago, an airline ran a clever national television advertising campaign that made fun of the idealistic, unrealistic world of air travel that airlines had pictured in their ads for years. They showed parody ads that featured singing flight attendants bringing never-ending trays of glorious food and drink to passengers who were all being treated like royalty.

Then you saw that the parody commercial was being shown on a television monitor in the gate area of an airport, being viewed by a bone-tired traveler whose flight was delayed yet again. It was a dismal scene that those of us who are airline road warriors could immediately relate to. The announcer then said, "Wouldn't it be great if air travel was like the commercials." It was a wonderfully creative ad that acknowledged that just because a commercial said that things were great didn't make them great, and that the customer can always see through the smoke and mirrors of advertising.

Brands are not created by commercials. Brands are created by ticket agents, and flight attendants, and baggage handlers, and pilots, and customer service representatives. Brands are created by every single employee in your company. Brand is not created by advertising agencies.

Inconsistency—The Great Brand Killer

Do you ever do business with a company that should hang a big sign outside their door that says "Feel Lucky? Then Come On In!"? You know, those companies that sometimes give great service, sometimes merely acceptable service, and sometimes no service at all? It's a common occurrence for most of us. You just hope that whomever you come in contact with is one of the good ones. It depends who you get. This one is a winner every time. That one will do a good job if you catch him in a good mood. And this one over here, well, if you get her then you're in for a bad experience.

Here's an example of how you can have people with the same jobs, working for the same company, literally standing side by side wearing the same uniforms, and have the desired brand being built and protected by one while the other is simultaneously tearing it down. I was in a taxi running late to catch a flight from Dayton, Ohio, to Chicago. I needed to make the flight so that I could be at a meeting with a client that evening.

The flight was scheduled to depart at 5:17 P.M. I got out of the taxi at the airport at about 5:12 P.M. Not good. I knew that my chances of making the flight were slim to none but I was determined to give it my best shot. I rushed up to the ticket counter where there were two airline employees on duty. One had a customer while the other was free. I ran up to the unoccupied ticket agent and explained that I was late for the 5:17 flight to Chicago, I had a ticket, and just needed a boarding pass as quickly as possible.

The ticket agent looked at her watch, turned to look at the listings of the flights on the board behind her, turned back to me and said, "I'm sorry sir, but you're really late."

"I know that." I said. "I just told you I was late. What I need is for you to get me a boarding pass so I can get to the gate." She looked at me with sincere empathy and said "Sir, I'm sure they've already called for final boarding for that flight. There's no way you can make that one. But we have another flight to Chicago in about 90 minutes and I'm sure I can get you a seat on that one."

At this point, the ticket agent standing next to her, who had obviously been listening to this exchange, turned to her customer and said "Sir, your flight doesn't leave for over an hour. Do you mind if I help this gentleman?" Her customer said he didn't mind at all, so she turned to me and said "Give me your ticket, quick!" She then printed out a boarding pass, slapped it on the counter, looked at me and with a definite sense of urgency said, "Here's your boarding pass. Your gate is at the end of the concourse. Now go! Go! Go!"

I didn't have the time to do what I wanted to do at that moment, which was look at both of the ticket agents and say "Let's examine what just happened here, shall we?"

I grabbed the boarding pass, turned, and ran for my gate as fast as I could. When I got within sight of my gate, there was good news and bad news. The bad news was that everyone had boarded and the waiting area was empty. The good news is that the plane was still at the gate and the jetway was still against the plane.

Again, there were two airline employees. One was finishing up paperwork at the gate desk, the other was walking toward me. I ran up to the one walking my way and said, "This flight . . . to Chicago . . . I'm late but I've got a boarding pass . . . and the plane is still there. Just open that door and get me on the plane and we're in business." The gate agent looked out the window at the plane, looked at her watch, turned back to me and said, "Sir, you're really late." In disbelief I said, "I know. We were just talking about that downstairs. But now I'm here. The plane's here. And all I need is for someone to let me on the plane."

She looked out the window at the plane again, and in a truly sympathetic voice said, "Sir, I'm sorry. Let me explain our policy. You see the reason you think the plane is still here is because you can see it there. But once we do our final boarding call and close that door, we can't let anyone else on the plane. We have another flight to Chicago in about 90 minutes, though." I don't know about you, but I'm not giving up until I run out of people.

I quickly go to my last chance, the airline employee at the desk. At this point, I'll readily admit that I was wound pretty tight and I did a bit of a frustration dump on the guy. I unleashed a rant asking how in the world an airline could have a plane sitting at the gate, not moving, with a very frequent flying customer standing less than a hundred feet away, and not be able to get the customer on the plane. He held up both hands in a calming motion and said, "Hey, there's no problem here, sir. They're not going anywhere without you. Come on." He then headed toward the door to the jetway.

On our way to the plane, he explained that this flight was waiting to load some baggage from a late connecting flight, and that we had a few minutes before they'd push back. He put me on the plane, I found a seat, and I began to reflect on what had just happened.

What happened was a classic case of a brand at serious risk. You can advertise 24 hours a day, and you can have some superstars as employees. But to the degree that you have people in the organization that do not fulfill the promise you make to the marketplace, you have what could very well be a critical weakness in the brand.

Category of One companies understand the ongoing nature of building, protecting, and communicating the brand all the time, 24/7.

Focus, Focus, Focus

To maintain brand strength requires focus and constant reinforcement with everyone in the organization. Brand isn't your mission statement and it isn't a 10-point list of priorities. Your brand should be a simple understanding of who you are, what you promise the marketplace, and your ability and willingness to keep that promise. The simpler the brand statement, the better.

At Quill, Larry Morse says that the essence of their brand is that they are "dedicated to providing customers with the very best service possible. If the customer is not happy for any reason, we will do whatever it takes to make things right." Morse says, "Quill's mission is simple: Treat our customers better than anyone else. That's what we have done for more than 46 years, and that is what our organization will always be totally focused on." That's the key. You pick one thing and you stay totally focused on it.

R.J. Young Company, a leading supplier of copiers and office machinery, has a similar brand concept. I'm a customer of R.J. Young, and I can personally testify that their idea of what they want their brand to be matches their advertising, and, most importantly, what their customers see as being the brand. For years, they have stated that "we'll make it right." Period. Forget what the warranty says. They want to know what *you* say will make you happy. "We'll make it right" truly is their brand.

When CST went through the process of determining the strengths they possessed that would take them to the next level, they kept coming back to the same thing. They realized that even though they were in a very technical business, their great strength was the quality of the relationships that they were able to create with customers, partners, and employees. Thus, the goal for their brand became a simple statement of "Our mission is you."

Communicate, Communicate, Communicate

Bobby Bradley of CST says that reinforcing their strength of relationships as the core of their rebranding effort was a process, not an event. "First of all, we had our managers as part of the process." Bradley says. "That was probably the biggest way we got buy-in. When we started, we interviewed them, told them what we were going to do, got their input, and got them thinking about our strengths. The key was keeping them involved along the way. We showed them that we value their opinions—some of their input we used—some of their concerns we took to heart."

Bradley says that by going with a strength they already had, the brand idea was an easy sell to the employees. She says "The other reason it was easy to get the buy-in from the general employee population was because these are things we're already doing. So it was easy to talk about it all. The language wasn't complicated. The ideas were easy to grasp. It's been received very well. Because we can compliment our staff and say you guys are already doing this and now we want to brag on you."

The constant reinforcement and communication of the brand to the employees in CST's rebranding effort took many forms. Every employee received a "Launch Card," which discussed the brand and why it was so important. Communicating the message to employees in person, especially by Bradley herself, was critically important. Focusing on the brand in the company newsletter, launching a new Web site, a new employee portal, and having all managers talking about the brand message were all important parts of the effort.

Bradley says that CST is making a significant investment in making the brand real. "We are now coming up with ways to reinforce the brand everywhere we can, in our awards programs, for example. We may bring key people in to the corporate office for face time with the senior folks for information sharing, training, just getting to know the company even better, maybe on a quarterly basis. Now that's going to cost us. But it's important and we're going to make room for it in the budget. We have to make sure our people know they're important to us. We have to mean it. Provide constant feedback."

Customers agreed that relationships were what the CST brand was all about.

Bradley says, "We got some spontaneous confirmation from our customers about 'Our Mission Is You,' while on our brand rollout trips. One customer said 'This is great—this is exactly who you are.' We were able to tell our employees about the compliments. Some customers said they couldn't do business without us. Often the customers were saying we're going to figure out how to keep you." When the customer's perception of brand is in synch with your intention for the brand you've got brand strength.

Brand Is Personal

Make no mistake, CST's product is information technology services, ranging from network management, software engineering, and data center management, to product procurement, systems engineering, and logistics services. But their product isn't their brand. They realized that their brand, their promise to the marketplace, wasn't technical. It was personal.

As CST puts it, "A job well done means more than just doing great work. It means doing great work in a way that builds successful relationships—with customers, employees, and partners. People are at the heart of what we do. Principles are at the heart of how we do business."

In their rebranding process, CST identified five basic principles of now they wanted to do business. All of these principles came from the idea of building a customer-focused technology company. CST's commitment to customers, its brand promise, is expressed through these principles.

The CST Brand: Our Mission Is You

Your mission becomes their mission. CST feels that the better they understand their customers' goals, the better they can assist them in accomplishing those goals. They make it a priority to take the time to learn the mission, functions, and operations of a customer's organization, as well as their goals for success. They then focus their management, technical, and administrative support efforts on achieving mission success as the customer defines it.

CST feels that a key to their brand is saying "yes" to customers as often as possible. Although they have large company capabilities, they work very hard at creating and maintaining the flexibility of a small company. Accommodating special requests has become an integral part of the brand promise.

Making the brand personal is the motivation behind CST's promise that their doors really are open to customers. Their brand promise includes access to their entire management organization, right up to company President Bobby Bradley. It's this kind of "promise keeping" that enables you to transcend product and service, and build a brand based on relationships.

Not by Accident

It takes an ongoing commitment to brand to take yours to the Category of One level. It doesn't happen by accident. Once brand takes hold, however, with proper attention it becomes the essence of who you are and what you do. It transcends policy, which enables you to transcend commodity. Brand becomes the way you do everything, almost without thinking.

Since I travel so much in my work, I have lots of brand experiences, good and bad, with the travel and hospitality industry. I experienced two great examples of brand strength in Marriott hotels, one in south Florida, one in Los Colinas, Texas. In the Florida Marriott, I was at the front desk to check on a package that was being shipped to me. There was one desk clerk on duty and I was her only customer. While she was on the phone checking on the status of my package, a customer walked up to the desk to check in.

While still on the phone she immediately acknowledged the new customer with a nod and a "Hello, sir, someone will be right with you." She then turned to press a button on the wall behind her, and another desk clerk immediately came to take care of the new guest.

A tiny action that spoke volumes about the brand. And it didn't happen by accident. This was very much by design, and happened so smoothly and naturally that it was obviously part of who they are. I asked the desk clerk about what she had done and with a smile she said, "We don't like for anyone to wait." Simple. Powerful.

Brand Means Remembering the Point

At the Los Colinas Marriott, I experience top to bottom brand strength the likes of which I have seldom seen in any company. It all culminated in the hotel restaurant where not only did I receive excellent service, but noticed a hotel manager in a suit circulating through the restaurant with an eye on everything that was happening. He made his way unobtrusively through the room, taking the time to speak to each customer while he helped the wait staff clear tables or deliver orders.

When he made his way to my table and asked if everything was satisfactory, I told him how impressed I was with not only the performance of his staff, but that he was taking such a personal interest and involvement in everything. He told me that he learned a long time ago that he was much more effective as a manager and leader when he spent as much time as possible with the employees and the customers instead of tucked away back in his office. "The point of my job isn't paperwork," he said. "The point of my job is to keep you happy, and to keep my employees happy so that they can do the best possible job of serving you."

More Than a Cup of Coffee

Earlier in this chapter, I told the story of how Starbucks had pulled me in and gotten my business with its brand power. But what is the Starbucks brand? Is it coffee? To some of their customers, I'm sure that the quality of Starbucks coffee is the brand. But Starbucks is much more than product. It's an atmosphere they create with their big, cushy furniture and their Internet connections for customer use. It's the music they play and the invitation to stay as long as you like to work, read, talk with a friend, or just stare into space over that afternoon mocha.

The real key to a strong brand, however, always comes back to the people. The challenge for a Starbucks is whether or not they can extend their brand strength beyond the cushy interior to, for instance, the drive-through window. Regular Starbucks' customer Kelly Weathers had a particularly brand-strengthening drive-through experience that he shared with me.

"This morning," Kelly said, "I was coming to the office about 6:00 A.M. and stopped by the local Starbucks. I don't know if you drink Starbucks," Kelly told me, "but you may after you hear this story. They not only have the best coffee, but you're going to love this."

"I pulled into the drive-through," he continued, "and a female voice came on and said, 'I'm sorry, but we do not open until 6:30, but I would be more than happy to brew some coffee for you if you have about two minutes.' Taken aback, I said 'No, that's okay,' and she said, 'I really don't mind,' so I pulled to the window. There stands this woman named Ann, probably no more than 22 or 23 years old. She even asked me what kind of coffee I wanted, traditional or mild."

"Trust me, it gets better." Kelly said. "So in no more than two minutes, which seemed like 15 seconds, she come to the window with the biggest cup of mild coffee they have. She did not ask me what size I wanted, she just gave me the large, which is what I would have ordered anyway. She asks me if I wanted cream and sugar, puts just cream in at my request and hands me the coffee and then she says, 'It's on the house!' "

"Can you believe that?" Kelly exclaimed. "Not only did she brew coffee for me 30 minutes before they opened, she did not even want me to pay for it. I gave her $5 and told her to keep the change and asked for her manager's name and store number. I have sent Starbucks' headquarters a letter and will send her manager a letter as well."

Remember that earlier in this chapter I said that it should be the top priority of every employee to build, protect, and represent your brand to the best of their ability. We just experienced

Ann, the Starbucks' employee, giving us a lesson. And it doesn't mean giving away the store. But once in a while, give away a piece of the store. It can come back in customer loyalty many times over.

Our Brand Is Cool

For many years, BMW has been remarkably consistent with its brand promise—sporty, dynamic, quality cars. As BMW has broadened its brand message to encompass the experience of owning a BMW, rather than just the product itself, the Bavarian automaker undertook what many saw as a risky branding effort—producing a collection of five short films that could be downloaded from the Internet.

BMW's sales growth in recent years has been good, but they wanted to make sure that they didn't suffer the fate of many luxury carmakers, who are seeing the average age of their customers inexorably climbing. Economic factors created a growing market of young auto buyers who wanted a luxury car, but they wanted "cool," as well as quality.

BMW wanted to target this market of customers between the ages of 25 and 44.

The question was how to reach them with an honest brand message that would convey more than the quality of the product. BMW has long been an automaker that connected emotionally with its buyers more deeply than most of its competitors. It wanted to continue this connection with younger buyers.

The challenge was that the media savvy market that BMW wanted to reach would be completely turned off if it perceived the films as just being commercials or nothing more than

"product placement films" for BMW. This would have created a branding backlash that could have completely torpedoed
the efforts to reach the market. BMW succeeded. The brilliance of what BMW achieved with its film collection, called
The Hire, is evidenced on many fronts.

The Medium *Is* the Message

The films are content driven, remarkably entertaining, and
showcase the autos themselves as being technologically advanced, incredibly cool, and almost painfully hip.

The delivery system for the films is equally brilliant.
BMWfilms.com created a DVD-like experience for the viewer.
Millions of young viewers in the target market went to the site
and downloaded the films. During the initial core promotion
for the films, they were viewed more than 11 million times,
exceeding BMW's expectations. Ultimately, the films were also
released on DVD, taking the campaign to even more potential
BMW buyers.

Now here's a key when thinking about the branding ramifications of the project. Not only are the films totally cool,
but the delivery system is equally cool. The Internet was used
as a marketing tool perhaps more effectively than ever before.
The mere fact that BMW was so technologically "with it" had
built-in appeal to the target market. The medium truly became part of the message. BMW's technological savvy became
part of the brand.

The promotional campaign to drive people to the
BMWfilms.com Web site was a cross-media effort. CNN,
ABC World News Tonight, Access Hollywood, USA Today,
the *New York Times, Entertainment Weekly,* and *Time*

magazine all did stories on the films. Guerilla public relations generated a buzz on the Internet and print advertising was strategically placed to reach the target market, including ads for the films in the Friday night movie listings. The BMWfilms.com Web site itself included still images, flash animations, streaming video, and streaming audio, all of which was welcomed with open arms by the young people who had been waiting for some company somewhere to do something cool with Internet marketing. And the ultimate appeal was that it didn't feel like marketing. It was just a collection of five great little movies.

Who's Who

The whole project was to convey the BMW brand as being cool, hip, exciting, and technologically advanced. Just as with their cars, BMW didn't skimp when it came to the quality of the talent they assembled for the film project. They brought together a virtual Who's Who collection of film directors and movie stars.

John Frankenheimer is an Emmy and Academy Award winner who has been directing films for five decades. Ang Lee's BMW film was his follow up to the Academy Award winning *Crouching Tiger, Hidden Dragon*. Lee was also the director of the popular film *Sense and Sensibility*. Guy Ritchie's box office hits include *Lock, Stock, and Two Smoking Barrels* and *Snatch* with Brad Pitt. Ritchie also brought along his wife Madonna to co-star in his BMW effort.

Director Alejandro Gonzalez Inarritu's first film, *Amoros Porros,* was nominated for Academy and Golden Globe Awards for best foreign film. Wong Kar-Wai won Best Director at the

1997 Cannes Film Festival for *Happy Together,* and he wrote the screenplay for the *Final Victory.*

Actor Clive Owen played the same character (The Driver) in each of the five movies. Owen was first seen by most American audiences in the critically acclaimed 1998 film *Croupier.* This film, by the way, is extremely cool. It's cool to the point that I bought a copy of it. Owen has since co-starred in *The Bourne Identity* with Ben Affleck and was a lead in Robert Altman's *Gosford Park.*

Did They Sell Any Cars?

BMW brought in very, very Big Guns to ensure that these weren't just quality films, but that they were very, very cool films. You might be thinking that it's all well and good to make a bunch of "cool" little films, but what's the point? The point is to sell cars. And how did the BMW films do in selling cars? BMW saw tremendous increases in most brand measures among the target market. A 77 percent increase was achieved among those from the target audience who saw the campaign that BMW was a brand "for people like me." Purchase receptivity rose among the target audience, and a triple-digit increase in planned dealer visits was achieved. Ultimately, 2001 sales jumped by 12.5 percent compared to 2000 without the benefit of any major product launches. BMW sales surpassed the 200,000 mark for the first time in history.

The films were released in April. That year BMW recorded its best May and June ever in terms of car sales, exceeding the 40,000-vehicle mark—despite a troubled economy. BMW was utterly thrilled with the results of this truly out-of-the-box branding effort. Thrilled to the point that BMW had three more spy thrillers in production within a year of the initial release of the five original films.

I Want One of Those

And what does all of this mean to you and me and our own attempts to become a Category of One brand? Just everything. Just that your brand has to be about what outcome you create for your customers. Your brand has to be about a feeling. Your brand has to be something that makes people say, "I want one of those," even if your product is paper clips or drill presses or socks or helicopters.

The lesson that BMW teaches us is that we have to do more than advertise a product and a price to create a strong brand. We have to tell a story about what it's like to do business with us. We have to convey to people with everything we do that there is a consistently good feeling that goes along with being our customer. And we have to convey that feeling with every single contact that our customer or potential customer has with us, be it through our employees, our ads, our Web sites, or our storefronts.

A Promise Kept

Larry Morse of Palm Harbor Homes believes that brand strength ultimately means you keep your promise. "Our brand stands for quality, durability, satisfaction, and energy efficiency," Morse says. "This has been true since our beginning. This consistency is one of our strengths and helps us clearly communicate to our customers and our associates our value proposition."

Improving the reputation of manufactured housing is also a brand goal for Palm Harbor Homes. "Our industry is known as 'marginal housing for marginal buyers,' " Morse says. "Our approach is customized quality housing for creditworthy buyers at monthly costs equivalent to apartment rent. Our systems, goals, compensation, measurements, advertising, and hiring profiles are all consistent with this contra view of the industry."

"We view brand building as enduring; therefore, the brand should be build on enduring values. Our 'marketing' of this brand is remarkably similar to our internal customers (associates) and to our external retail customers. In the end, 'More Home for Your Money' better mean something real or our people and our customers will soon see it as just a slogan and not a promise kept.

Brand is everything. One more time: It should be the top priority of every employee to build, protect, and represent your brand to the best of their ability.

The
Three Rules

Customer Rules

Rule 1: Know more about the customer than anyone else.

Rule 2: Get closer to the customer than anyone else.

Rule 3: Emotionally connect with the customer better than anyone else.

Every Category of One company excels at following and living these three rules. In a customer-driven market, which we are in and will be in for the foreseeable future, there are no substitutes for knowing more about, getting closer to, and emotionally connecting with the customer.

The Greatest Competitive Advantage

The three customer rules are actions that take place simultaneously, because when you know more about the customer than anyone else, you have the ability to get closer than anyone else, and you then begin to connect emotionally. Combining these three actions will give you the single greatest competitive advantage in business. Nothing else can enable you to transcend commodity and defy comparison. Assuming that you are competitive at the commodity level, meaning with price, product quality, and service, the three customer rules are the most powerful way to become a Category of One company.

It Starts with Knowing More

I have always remembered something taught by the great sales trainer Tom Hopkins who said that your first goal as a salesman is to have the customer "like you and trust you." I tend to agree with this idea, but it's not the starting point. Having the customer like and trust you is what happens when you get closer and establish an emotional connection. The process begins with knowing more about that customer.

I often work with sales professionals who are all interested in how they can close more sales. What I tell them isn't what most of them want to hear, because it's not the magic bullet phrase or the presentation technique that is an easy shortcut to making the sale. The single most powerful sales tool, assuming that you are competitive at the commodity level, is to know more about the customer going in.

The problem with this idea in the eyes of many is that it takes too much time. They have to be out making sales calls and simply don't have the time to research and know more about these potential customers. I hope that my competitors have the same attitude. It makes my job incredibly easy.

How Could They Not Know?

A few years ago, I had the opportunity to offer a proposal to a bank. The bank had contacted two other consultants as well with a request for a proposal on working with all of their branch managers on ways to increase their retail market share. The bank specifically wanted to hear our proposals verbally, rather than have them in written form. I was informed that the selection committee at the bank would interview each of us separately on a conference call, during which we were to put forth our proposal. The calls were to take place on a Monday in two weeks.

I prepared my proposal for a program to help the bank increase retail market share, felt good about it, and looked forward to the Monday conference call. I knew that I would be the last of the three consultants to be interviewed that day when the call came through in mid-afternoon. The committee was on a speakerphone in one of the bank's conference rooms, and after initial introductions around the table, I was asked to present my proposal.

"First things first," I said. "This is not the time for you to be thinking about increasing market share. You have many customers out there, particularly your older customers, who are going to be very nervous and wondering whether they should stay with you or move their business to a competitor. You need to be focusing on retaining the market share you've got. You also have a bank full of employees who are going to be even more nervous than your customers. When they read in the newspaper on Saturday morning that you had been sold to a bigger bank, then their world became a giant question mark. With this surprise sale, you've got some immediate issues to deal with that I think I can help you with."

There was a very long silence at the bank's end of the phone line. I thought to myself, "Well, it looks like this one bit the dust." The voice of the chairperson of the selection committee came over the phone. "Mr. Calloway, you've got the job. Let's talk about what we need to do." We then proceeded to discuss the new issues that were on the table in light of the sale of the bank, and how we should best proceed in terms of initial damage control, and then the creation of opportunity.

My favorite part of the conversation came when one of the bankers interrupted the conversation with a question for me. "Mr. Calloway," he said, "I'm curious about one thing. How could the other consultants not know? They didn't even know that we had been sold. It was all over the business news all weekend. How could they not know?" "Quite honestly," I replied, "I have no earthly idea how they could not know."

Sometimes winning is so easy that it doesn't seem fair. Sometimes it's like bobbing for water.

Sales Calls versus Customer Knowledge

I've been in the business speaking and consulting field long enough to have earned a bit of an "Old Pro" status with people new to the industry. I'm often asked to speak to groups of professional speakers and consultants about how they can build their business. Like everyone else, they want to know how to get more sales. Like everyone else, few of them want to hear my "know more about the customer" philosophy. Like everyone else, they say they're too busy making sales calls.

Let's look at a typical selling situation in my business. I received an e-mail from a guy who was looking for someone to speak to his company's annual managers' meeting. He wanted to know if we could schedule a phone call to talk about what I might do. He made it clear that he was in the very preliminary stages of finding a speaker, and that he was contacting a number of potential speakers. I wrote back explaining that my approach at this stage was to help determine whether or not I was a good fit for his company, and that if I felt I wasn't, that I would be the first to tell him and would help him find someone who was.

This is, in fact, my whole approach in the initial stages of the selling process. I never try and talk someone into doing business with me. I find out whether it makes sense for both of us to work together. If it does, fine. The sale takes place quite naturally. If it doesn't, that's also fine. It would be very damaging to my business if I were to try and make myself fit into a situation where I'm not right for the job. I do not want to be a square peg trying to fit into a round hole.

The subsequent phone call opened with the guy saying, "Joe, I don't know how much you know about our company, but it's important that whoever we choose understand us and what we're going through right now." "Let me tell you what little I do know," I said. "I know that you are wanting to come out of this period of bankruptcy with a sense that it's a new day, and you want to convey that idea both internally to your managers and externally to your customers. I know that you are reorganizing your entire sales organization, and my guess is that this will be the major focus of the upcoming managers' meeting. I know that your competitor is beating you on price, but that the value you bring to the table in terms of the research you do and how that benefits your customers still makes you extremely competitive. I know that because of your strength in research and knowledge that you should be selling solutions, not products. I know that your new CEO has got a strong background in successful turnaround projects, and that he brings a strength in operations and sales that you've not had before. But it's important to me that I find out much more. What I'd like to do is fly to your headquarters on my own dime and spend a day with you and your people so that I have a really good handle on your situation, exactly what you want to accomplish at this meeting, and how I might be able to help you if we both feel it's a good match." His reply was short and sweet. "Joe, you've got the job."

Many new people in my profession and even some of my experienced competitors will tell me that they don't have time to do that kind of research and certainly can't take the time and spend the money to fly out to talk with a prospective customer. They've got to stay on the phone making cold calls. Fine. You guys dial for dollars. I'll know more about the customer. I'll win every time.

Your Job Is Knowledge

My job is to understand business, how business works, and how I can help my clients be more successful. Some of my competitors think that their job is giving speeches or writing books. Speeches and books are just the delivery systems for what I really do, which is know more. The discipline I follow, and I do consider it a discipline, in gaining competitive advantage knowledge is a simple one that takes place on two levels.

The first level is what I consider to be ongoing awareness knowledge about the marketplace in general. I read everything. I mean that almost literally, especially when it comes to periodicals. I am a magazine and newspaper junkie. Certainly when it comes to knowing what's happening in business, I read most of what I consider to be the good, general sources of information including *Forbes, Fortune,* the *Wall Street Journal, BusinessWeek,* and about a dozen other general business publications. I also go to many business news Web sites and visit corporate Web sites on an almost daily basis.

When I research a company in preparation for an initial sales discussion, I'll cover the basics including annual reports, articles that may have been written on the company in the past year, and any company newsletters or internal publications that they will send me. The secret weapon, however, is the company Web site. And the secret weapon within that company's Web site is the section with "news and press releases." That will bring you up to speed on what's happening right now with the company.

When you combine the ongoing market awareness research with the targeted company research, which the Internet makes ridiculously easy and time efficient, then it's just a complete no-brainer to get the knowledge. So many people say they don't have the time to research and prepare. I say I don't have the time to waste on sales calls and presentations with a low likelihood of turning into business. I don't have the slightest inclination to try and do business with a customer that I'm not a good match for. If I do enough of those I'm out of business anyway.

We're Here to Give Them What They Want

When we first opened Mirror, the restaurant in which I'm a partner in Nashville, Tennessee, our menu was mostly a selection of *tapas* dishes. *Tapas* is a Spanish word meaning small bites, or small plates. It was basically appetizer-size dishes that customers could order a variety of and have with a glass of wine to make up a complete meal. Great idea and great food. And our customers didn't want it. They loved the food, that wasn't the problem. They didn't like the tapas concept.

Luckily, at Mirror we have two great partners in our chef, Michael DeGregory, and our manager, Colleen DeGregory. Colleen said it best when she declared, "We're not here to educate our customers about dining. We're here to give them what they want." So we changed the menu and the rest, as they say, is history. The restaurant took off and has developed a loyal following of customers who we work very hard to understand so that we can give them what they want. Our business is knowledge. In the restaurant business, our job is to understand our customers so that we can give them what they want, a total dining experience that makes them happy. Our job is knowledge.

So is yours. That you have a great quality product and excellent service at a competitive price is a given. That's all on the commodity level. To transcend commodity, you have to go to the next level and the best door into that level is knowledge of the customer. It's very dangerous to assume that you know what the customer wants or to take what you think is your competitive advantage and try and force it on the customer. What you think is an advantage might well be what the customer thinks is a disadvantage.

He Guessed Wrong

I was called on by a salesman for a men's clothing business that specialized in coming to your office with swatches of material, from which you could pick what you wanted, get measured, and have suits or shirts designed and delivered within a few weeks. The salesman had a pitch. That was his mistake. He had a prepared sales pitch that was based on guessing that he knew what I wanted.

The salesman told me that a busy man like me didn't have time to go into a store and wade through racks full of suits or shelves packed with shirts. With his service, I could sit in the comfort of my own office and quickly thumb through his material samples to make a selection quickly and conveniently. No muss. No fuss.

He guessed wrong.

I explained to him that what he was presenting as a supposed advantage was the exact opposite of the experience that I was looking for. What I like to do when I'm shopping for clothes is to go to a great store, with great people and great furnishings, and, above all, a salesperson who knows me very well, and I like to take my time. A busy guy like me finds it relaxing and a pleasure to slowly appreciate the selection of suits and shirts and not feel rushed. Besides, it gives me a chance to get out of the office.

He Paid Attention

Contrast that experience with Mike Barrett, who I've bought clothes from for years. While I go to a number of different clothing stores around town, I tend to go back to Mike time after time for one reason. He knows me better than his competition. It didn't happen by accident. Over the years, Mike has paid close attention to what I like and how I want to do business. I might also add that over the years those things have changed, as they do for most people.

Mike calls me when the black Italian suits come in. Mike calls me when the classically styled ties come in. Mike calls me when the white French cuff shirts come in. Mike knows me. Mike knows that when I come into the store he can wave, say hi, and leave me alone. Because Mike knows that I have very definite opinions about what I like and that I'm perfectly happy to browse for a long time. I'll pick what I want and then signal for help with the fitting. If I want Mike's advice on a tie or shirt or anything else, I'll ask and he'll be there in a flash and do a great job of advising me.

Mike isn't focused on what he wants to sell. Mike is focused on who he is selling to. And that gets him closer to me. The knowledge comes first, the closeness comes next.

The bonus of getting as much knowledge about the customer as quickly as possible is that it helps you avoid getting into situations that wouldn't work for either party.

Nice to Meet You—Thanks for Your Time

Category of One performers are very good at knowing where they fit and where they don't. They'll walk away from a bad fit quickly. They focus on gaining knowledge not for the purpose of making a sale, but for the purpose of seeing if it's a good fit. The worst thing you can do for your business long term is to get outside of what you're good at and try and do a job that someone else should be doing.

I met with a gentleman who, through a mutual friend, had asked for an appointment to discuss with me some investment opportunities. I was on the lookout for good investments that would fit with my overall plan and so I agreed to meet with him. It was one of the more impressive sales calls I've ever experienced.

He opened by giving me one concise sentence describing the kind of investment work that he did. He followed that statement with a question, asking me to describe my overall financial plan and approach to investing. I responded with my own simple statement about what I wanted to accomplish and how. He said "Mr. Calloway, you're on the right track for what you want to do. The type of investment that I handle wouldn't be a good fit with your plan. It was nice to meet you. Thanks for your time."

Perfect. He was a professional who understood where he fit and he had no desire to try and force himself into a situation where he didn't fit. He didn't waste my time or his by giving me a long pitch about how he was the answer to everybody's problems. And because he had such respect for my time, he earned my appreciation. I have since referred three people to him because I felt that they might be a great fit with what he had to offer.

Try the Fries

Our restaurant, Mirror, has some unique dishes that most people aren't familiar with. Something on our menu might send them into a state of nirvana but it would never occur to them to order it. One of our waiters, Nick, does a great job of making suggestions to people about what we might have that they'd like. He does this after having gathered enough information about the customer, which might include the drink they order or a question they ask about the menu, to make an educated guess about what to suggest. This is a very different approach from the canned pitch where you make the assumption that everyone will want everything you suggest. Nick changes his suggestions based on who he's waiting on.

One of our signature dishes is the blue cheese polenta fries. They are so good that the Food Network actually did a program on our restaurant featuring the fries. Now when most people see blue cheese polenta fries on the menu, they usually have no idea what they are, and if they make a guess, they are likely to eliminate them as a choice because of assumptions about blue cheese, polenta, or fries. But if we think you are the kind of customer who might enjoy them, and most of our customers tend to be pretty adventurous and sophisticated diners or they wouldn't come to us in the first place, we suggest them. Almost without fail, customers absolutely love the blue cheese polenta fries and are thrilled that we suggested them. But the key is knowing the customer well enough to suggest them with confidence.

It's Not the Customer's Job

One of the classic customer relationship mistakes is to assume that because you've asked your customer if there's anything else you can do to help them, that you're doing a good job of fulfilling their needs. The problem with relying on customer feedback to find out what they want is that the customer may have absolutely no idea what you have available that would either solve a problem or make them happy.

I said as much to my former banker a few years ago when she called on me as a part of a "get close to our customers" program. She visited me at my office, for the first time ever, I might add, with a checklist to go through that would demonstrate to me, the customer, that the bank really, really cared about me and wanted to get close.

After going through her canned pitch on what basic services the bank offered, she went through the status of my current accounts and business with the bank. Gee, thanks for taking my time to tell me what my balances are and that I pay all my loans off on time and that I'm a good customer. I knew that already. She then concluded her visit with a grand gesture of cementing our "close" relationship. "Is there anything else that we can do for you?" she asked.

Well, how on earth should I know? I'm not a banker. And, particularly in this day of financial services when banks are getting into all kinds of services that they never used to offer, what makes her think that I would have a clue what they can do? The services she had told me about were all the services I was already using. Instead of going through this charade of pretending to get closer to me, she should have spent the time asking me questions so that she would understand the business I was in and maybe develop an idea that could help me create an opportunity.

I have since fired that bank and moved all of my business to a much smaller bank where they truly do take the time to understand their customers and get closer through that knowledge. Running a marketing promotion in which you make a token visit and then simply declare that you're closer is just a waste of time for everyone.

Markets of One

All aspects of customer relationship management (CRM) are becoming very hot topics for businesses today. The technology exists to let most of us know more about our customers than ever before. This is a good thing as long as the information is used constructively. Too many companies are instituting elaborate CRM programs thinking that having more data on customers will be the silver bullet that solves all their problems and opens up the doors of growth and prosperity. It's a matter of knowing what to do with the knowledge once you get it. More data isn't necessarily better. Get the right data then know how to use it to get closer to your customers.

Many people say that the problem with the Internet is that it can't provide the personal service that face-to-face transactions provide. The people that say this obviously haven't done much shopping on the Internet. What the Internet can do is exactly what the excellent individual can do face-to-face— know who I am. That's the key. The days of marketing to a demographic model are over. If you are targeting male customers of a particular age who are in a certain income range and live in a specified geographic area, then you will probably lose to your competitor who is targeting me. Me. Joe Calloway. A marketing target of one.

This is what the Internet can do very effectively and it is what every business should be doing whether they have an Internet presence or not. Sell to markets of one. Get close to your customers one at a time, not one group at a time. Extraordinary companies have always done business this way and now we've reached the point that it's fast becoming an entry-level requirement.

Know Who I Am

A great chef was once asked what his favorite restaurant was. He said that his favorite restaurant was the one where they knew him. When I ask my audiences to name their favorite company and why, the most common reason is that the company knows them, calls them by name, remembers what they like, understands them, and can make recommendations based on that understanding. This is the point of customer relationship management, to understand the customer, know him, and get close to him.

I do a great deal of shopping over the Internet. When I go online to buy a book, the bookseller's home page comes up with a personal greeting to me, and has a list of books that I might be interested in. How do they know what to recommend to me? They use technology to remember what I buy and the kinds of books that I like. The corner bookstore can do the same with good people, if they are willing to invest the time and effort in making customer knowledge a priority.

Sometimes the Internet company will raise the bar even higher, letting me call a customer service representative on the phone and speak with them live while we are both looking at the same screen on our computers. She will explain the product to me and answer any questions that I might have, including making recommendations for a product that might better suit me. No personal service on the Internet? Think again.

Generic Won't Work

My former bank's idea of personal service was to send out a mass mailed newsletter written by some marketing company for banks everywhere to send to their customers as a cheap version of personalized attention. How bogus. Once upon a time this sort of thing made an impression on customers, but no more. The use of the generic newsletter or mailer is still popular among banks, insurance companies, and real estate companies, but the extraordinary ones are doing something that some would consider quite retro. They are going back to the truly individual version of communication done one customer at a time. Either through the use of technology, as in e-commerce, or simply through excellent individuals willing to invest the time in getting closer, generic marketing is getting trounced by One on One Marketing.

If your company is taking the generic approach to business, you would do well to consider how you might get closer to your customers one at a time. Are you like the branch of a telecommunications company that meets with a customer council once a quarter? Have you created a communications pipeline with customers that lets them tell you their stories good and, especially, bad? Do you have a process in place that gets you that information?

Do you have a way to find out what your customer's perception is of your company, its image, its advertising? Do you know what noncustomers think of you? Do you know what your competitor's customers think of you? Do you know what your competitors think of you? Would your customers make this statement about your company? "My account rep has made suggestions that improved our profitability or effectiveness."

If you're not doing these things, how in the world do you expect to get close enough to your customers to keep their business?

Losing Your Grip

There are many companies out there who would be very surprised if they could read the minds of some of their best customers. Here's what their customers are thinking: "You think that because we've been doing business with you for a long time that we're a sure thing. Well, we're looking around. We're getting the feeling that you've stopped hustling for our business. We get the feeling that you've got your eye on some new potential customers out there and that you're paying a lot of attention to them. Hey, your good thing's about to go bad. Because we will fire you. We will find somebody new. Somebody who treats us like we want to be treated. Somebody who after years and years of business will reward that loyalty and shower us with all the good things we deserve."

Departure signals are imminent. But many companies don't see them. They're so anxious to go out there and drum up new business that their best customers are about to walk out the back door. Today's customer will leave in a heartbeat if she thinks she's being ignored or taken for granted. Beware of the trap of trying to get close to new business when your old business is feeling neglected. Years ago, there was a commercial for an airline in which the president of a company gave out plane tickets to his entire salesforce. Each of them had been assigned an old customer to visit because one of their best and oldest customers had fired them on the grounds of neglect and being taken for granted.

The Emotional Connection

I often ask my clients if they believe that it's necessary to have an emotional connection with their customers. While some of them are surprised by the question, after a bit of thought, almost all of them agree that you do need to connect emotionally with customers, especially if you aim to defy comparison with your competitors. Most people will say that they want their customers to love doing business with them. If ever there was an emotion, surely it's love. It's extremely difficult to get to that Category of One status with your customers unless you create a strong emotional connection with them.

This principle holds true in any business. In my work with a group of concrete pipe manufacturers, I had them talk about the importance of connecting emotionally with their customers. These are guys who sell concrete pipe to government and commercial buyers. It's strictly a business-to-business marketplace. And yet every one of them recognized the value of connecting emotionally. One of them put it this way, "When everything else is pretty much equal, I need any edge I can get. If I have someone inside that company or government agency who is willing to go to bat for my company because he wants to work with us even if a competitor beats us on price, then that's an emotional connection."

All extraordinary companies understand the power of emotion. The short films BMW produced by some of the world's best movie directors are a great example of emotionally connecting with customers. The sole purpose was to connect BMW with customers and potential customers on an emotional level. You see the film and you want to experience the emotion that is conveyed and associated with the car. The films were cutting edge and helped BMW connect emotionally with people who would want a cutting edge automobile.

Michael Jordan is one of the most effective product endorsers in the history of marketing because of the emotional connection that he has with his fans. Companies wanted to transfer that emotional connection to their products through association with Michael. In the 1970s, Coke had a commercial featuring "Mean" Joe Greene, the great football player for the Pittsburgh Steelers, tossing his jersey to a young boy who had given Mean Joe a cold Coke after a game. It was pure emotion and it was selling a soft drink. There are many athletes who have achieved fame and fortune, but who aren't good candidates for product endorsement because there's no positive emotional connection between them and the public.

Think of the studios that have produced movies that you've seen over the years—Columbia, Universal, RKO, and United Artists. I'll bet that you can probably even recall some of their logos, like the woman holding the torch for Columbia, the radio tower for RKO, and the spinning globe for Universal. But I'd also bet that you don't really have any emotional feeling one way or another about any of those studios. You know them and they are famous brands, but they're all competitors in a category. None of them has achieved Category of One status.

Let me give you another name to consider. Disney. Almost everyone has an emotional connection with Disney. That emotional connection is what has made Disney a clear Category of One when it comes to movies. You not only have a judgment about the quality of their products, you also have a feeling that helps create an experience around their products. The question is what are you doing to create an emotional connection with your customers?

The Highest Level

Connecting emotionally with customers takes you to the highest level of business, where it becomes, as my friend and professional speaker Jim Cathcart says, "an act of friendship." This is as good as it gets. Not that you take it for granted at this point. To create and then sustain an emotional connection with customers takes ongoing attention and effort. The payoff is that you lock in customer loyalty.

You want to get to the point where when your customers are approached by a competitor with what could be considered a better deal at the commodity level of price, product quality, or service, that you transcend commodity and defy comparison in the mind of your customer. They simply can't hear what your competitor is saying. As long as you stay reasonably competitive at the commodity level, you have bulletproof customer loyalty.

Emotional connection is created over time, with a series of actions. It's almost always small actions that take place on a personal level. Disney employees waving at the passing train, Ritz Carlton employees who say hello to each guest as they pass them in the hallways, the orthodontist's staff that sends flowers, the computer service representative who remembers your kids' names and asks about them. It's tiny actions by regular people that create the most powerful force in business.

An emotional connection is created when, instead of sending a customer a generic mailing produced by a marketing company, you remember that she once expressed an interest in Japanese rock gardens, and you send her an article on the subject that you discovered while reading a magazine on a plane. It's created when you demonstrate an interest in him as a person and not just as a customer. It's created when you see an opportunity to help a customer solve a problem or create an opportunity in an unexpected way.

A Glass in the Box of Detergent

I remember when I was a kid that companies used to give you something extra to entice you to buy their product. They used to put a drinking glass, for example, in a box of detergent. Gas stations would give away a dishtowel when you filled your car up. I remember the Superman costume that my dentist gave me when I was about 4 years old. To this day, I give my current dentist, Dr. Cheryl Scott, a hard time about her not giving me a Superman costume.

I once gave a speech on customer service for the managers of a boat manufacturing company. The event was held on site at their manufacturing plant in the big meeting room. The presentation went extremely well, and made a great impression on the entire management team. After the presentation, a woman who was one of the company vice presidents approached me. She said that they had a driver ready to take me back to the airport and asked what time my flight was. I told her that I had about three hours to kill until the departure time.

She asked me if I remembered back in the 1950s and 1960s when they used to put a glass in the box of detergent. I smiled at the memory and told her that I certainly did. She said "I'm going to give you a chance to put a glass in the detergent box for us. We don't have any budget for this, but we've got a plant full of people back there making boats who never get to hear someone like you. If you would take even 30 minutes to speak with them in the meeting room, we'll shut down the plant to give them the opportunity. We think your message was that important. And we'd appreciate it more than you could possibly know."

Of course, I said yes, and had a wonderful time with the employees from the plant. And I definitely made an emotional connection with that client that lasts to this day. The interesting thing about the situation to me, though, was that not only did I connect with them, the client connected with me just in the act of asking me for the favor. Not only the receiver benefits in this kind of exchange, even if not for money. The giver often gets more.

I am constantly on the lookout for ways to put a glass in the box of detergent. Three days after the September 11, 2001, World Trade Center, Pentagon, and Pennsylvania disasters, I was scheduled to speak at a meeting of Executive Women International, who had decided to hold their convention as planned, in spite of the tragedy. It was an act of courage and an expression of strength on their part, especially when you remember that the airlines were grounded at that time, and their members had to drive from all across the country to attend the convention at the Opryland Hotel in Nashville, Tennessee.

I was scheduled to give the opening keynote speech and conduct two afternoon workshops on branding. After my opening speech, I was spending time talking with some of the coordinators of the event and I noticed that there seemed to be a buzz about some sort of problem. I asked what was going on and was told that their luncheon speaker hadn't shown up and they hadn't heard from her. This was understandable in the aftermath of the recent tragedy and was most likely due to the speaker's inability to travel. She had probably just forgotten to contact the group and tell them.

I said, "Look, I'm here and I'm not going anywhere. You've already heard me speak this morning and I've got two sessions to do for you this afternoon, but I want you to know that if you would like for me to, I'll be more than happy to do the lunch speech at no extra charge. I know that your attendance was understandably way down from what you had planned on because of the tragedy, and your budget for this meeting really took a hit from that." I have never seen such a look of relief on a group of faces in my life. I did the speech, their appreciation was overwhelming, and an emotional connection was made.

Was it smart business for me to do that? Sure. But more important, it was the right thing to do. It went way beyond business. This was a good group of people who needed some help and I was easily able to give them that help. That's what Jim Cathcart means when he says that business should be an act of friendship.

The New Customer Reality

Minimum Expectations

Today's incredible innovation is tomorrow's minimum expectation. A few years ago, hotel owners would have thought you'd lost your mind if you suggested that they put an iron and ironing board in every room. Today, it's expected. Computer power ports on airplanes, Internet connections in coffee shops, free oil changes and replacement tires that come as part of the deal with a new car, gas pumps that take virtually any credit card—all were crazy ideas that broke the rules. Then they were seen as great innovations. And quickly those crazy ideas became expected standards of performance. Customers' expectations are becoming greater every day, and there's no sign that they'll do anything but increase more rapidly in the future.

There's a new customer reality out there today. You can take that old cliché of customer service: "The customer's always right," and add a few things to it, not the least of which is the fact that today's customer is completely running the game and making up all the rules. One of the great challenges for any business today is dealing with this new customer reality. Category of One companies understand this reality and the attitude that today's customers bring to the table, and they use it to create new opportunities.

Mad as Hell

The customer used to know his place and generally took whatever the seller was willing to give him. And if he wasn't happy? Well, he pretty much kept it to himself. Things have changed. Boy, have they ever.

Remember the movie "Network"? Howard Beale was a respected network news anchor. Then one day he just snapped. He became the crazed, mad, ranting spokesman for a cynical and dissatisfied television-viewing public. He eventually gets people all over the country to get up, walk over to their windows, lean out, and scream "I'm mad as hell! And I'm not going to take it anymore!"

Lean out of your window and see if you hear anything. Hear that noise? Those are your customers you hear screaming out there. And not just your customers. Everybody's customers. Not only are they screaming, they're leaving. If you don't give them what they want, the way they want it, when they want it, it's over. You're dead meat. Road kill on the highway of business.

The old reality of business was that the seller was in control. It was the seller, the vendor, and the manufacturer, who always made up the rules. No more. Shifts in the economy, deregulation, and new technology have changed the balance of power. Now the customer rules. Today's customer has power like never before. And they are using it. There's a new sheriff in town. It's the customer.

Tough Customers—Tough Questions

Think of yourself and what you want as a customer, and then answer the following questions:

1. Are you a tougher customer than you were five years ago?
2. Are you a more informed and more educated buyer than you were five years ago?
3. Are you more likely to complain on the spot if you experience a problem?
4. Do you demand better service than you used to?
5. If you do not receive the service you want, are you more likely today to fire that business and never come back?
6. Are you more likely today to take action such as writing or calling a company's management with a complaint?
7. Do you tell more people today about companies that you have experienced problems with?
8. Do you take no for an answer or are you more likely to go up the chain of command until you get satisfaction?
9. Do you demand more value today than ever before for every dollar that you spend?
10. Do you feel like you have choices in who you do business with and that you will exercise those choices in a heartbeat if you don't get the service you want?

See? You're pretty tough yourself, aren't you? Well, your customers are at least as tough as you are.

The customers are mad as hell and they're not going to take it anymore! This new customer reality is scaring some businesses to death. They can't stand the thought of customers taking over.

But the smart businesses, those Category of One companies, the ones who can create opportunity regardless of which way the market winds blow, are those that come to the table of the marketplace and say, "Deal the cards. We're in." The key to success today is to open your doors, give your customers the keys, and say, "Here. You're the boss. Tell us what you want, and we'll give it to you."

Quality Is an Entry Level Factor

Consider this: The new reality is that it's not about quality anymore. Quality, meaning product quality, as a component in the whole concept of value, is so incredibly important that it has graduated from its past status as a competitive factor. It's an *expected* factor. Quality has become an expected factor because quality is everywhere. Everybody brings a quality product or service to the marketplace. If they don't, they disappear practically overnight.

Not long ago, I was speaking to an auto manufacturer's sales meeting at the McCormick Convention Center in Chicago. The Chicago Auto Show was about to open and we were talking about what customers expected and wanted and how to sell to them. I asked them to please understand that the auto show today is a totally different deal than it was a few years ago.

In the old days, people would go to an auto show and walk around all the different kinds of cars making comments like this:

"Wow. What a piece of junk."

"Garbage. More garbage. Wouldn't have it."

"Oooh, now there's a good car . . . that one over there . . . that's a good car."

"But look at these over here—junk, junk, junk, junk, junk, junk."

The point being that only about every ninth or tenth car was considered a quality, well-built automobile.

Today people walk in the auto show and what do they say? "Wow! Look at these babies! It's just one good car after another. Buick, BMW, Ford, Nissan, Chevy, Cadillac, Honda, Hyundai . . . good car, good car, good car, good car."

Everybody makes a good car now. It is the price of admission to the game. And it has revolutionized the car business because the playing field called quality has in fact become level. Think back to the so-called golden years of automobiles. When I first got my driver's license in the 1960s, there was a standard procedure that went with buying a new car. You bought the car, drove it for a few days, and then took it back to the dealer with all the things that were wrong and needed to be fixed. Nobody minded because we fully expected to buy a new vehicle with many little problems. Today, if you were sold a new car with that many problems, you'd drive it back right through the dealer's showroom window! Things today work! Tires can pick up a nail and go 50 miles with no air in them!! We expect quality. It is an entry-level factor in the value equation.

The Total Experience

What so many people in business today don't fully realize is that people don't buy just products anymore. I once asked a group of travel agency sales managers to each give an example of a great buying experience. One of them said that his happened at a bicycle store. He is a competitive racer and had spent over $4,000 on a bicycle. When asked what was so great about the buying experience, he said that the salesman was the only person he knew who loved bicycles more than he did. This particular salesman, he said, would call periodically after the sale to check and see if the bicycle was working out as expected, and he kept up with his customers' success in the different races. "The whole experience of doing business with this guy is much more than the bicycle. It's about my experience as the owner of the bicycle," he said.

Today the World Is Perfect

I had a similar experience with a car dealer. The new car I had bought at Thorobred Motorcars came with a built-in service plan that included periodic oil changes, beginning at 5,000 miles. Coincidentally, when I was about due for the first oil change, I noticed that the control knob for the mirror adjustment had been knocked off and had disappeared, and I also discovered a long, thin scratch down the side of the car.

I was about to leave town and was able to leave the car with the dealer for a few days if necessary, so I drove in that morning without having made a service appointment in advance. When the service manager approached me, I explained that I didn't have an appointment, didn't expect or need service that morning, and could easily wait a few days for the car. "No problem, Mr. Calloway," he said. "We'll get right on it." He took down the information about the oil change, the missing knob, and the scratch, then directed me to the courtesy van that would take me to my office. The van driver immediately appeared, greeted me by name, and quickly delivered me to the front door of my office building.

About two hours later, the service manager at Thorobred Motorcars called me and said, "Mr. Calloway, your car is ready, when would you like us to pick you up?" I asked if he was sure that everything had been taken care of, including the scratch. He assured me that it had. I told him that if the world was perfect, that I'd love for them to come pick me up immediately. "Today, Mr. Calloway, the world is perfect. We'll be right there," he said. Ten minutes later, the courtesy van appeared and whisked me to the dealer.

The service manager greeted me and said that all was taken care of and the car would be right up. I thanked him and asked how much I owed for the replaced knob and for repairing the scratch. "Why, there's no charge, Mr. Calloway," he said. "We're glad to do it." At that moment, a driver brought my car around, greeted me by name, thanked me for my business, and wished me a good day.

Thorobred Motorcars just went beyond product and transcended commodity.

Because I work with many auto manufacturers, I like to drive different makes of cars so that I can keep up with what's going on in that world among the different brands. My thoughts as I drove back to the office were that even though I might have no problem with driving another make of car after this one, I would sure miss doing business with this particular dealer. It wasn't the product that had hooked me, it was the total experience of doing business with them. It used to be that you went to a particular car dealer only because that's where you could get the brand of car you wanted. Now, with so many quality cars on the market, more of us will buy a particular kind of car to get to do business with the dealer that we want to do business with.

A bicycle, a guitar, a car, a cup of coffee, or any other product easily becomes a commodity in the eyes of the marketplace, and the only way some companies are able to compete or differentiate is with price. The problem with price is that it can be so easily met or beaten. Focusing on the customer and the ownership experience, however, becomes a differentiator that isn't easily matched.

Look around in almost any store—computers, televisions, stereos, can openers, you name it. One of the worst purchases you can make is to pay extra for the extended warranty on that new television or stereo you just bought. Why? Because it's going to last for years and years anyway! Things work so much better today than ever before.

Look at the difference in commercials today compared to just a few years ago. Take a commodity product like gasoline, for instance. A few years ago, almost every commercial for gasoline stressed quality. Secret formulas and great mileage and better acceleration were the kinds of things the gas companies talked about. But now everybody makes good quality gasoline. All the major gasoline companies know it. And they know that you know it. So they are now advertising what you are interested in, which is not the quality of the gasoline. That's a given. What people want to know is how you *buy* the gasoline because that's the competitive factor today—not the product, but the experience of buying the product.

What about price? Many people think that in business today the sun rises and sets based almost totally on price. But I have found that when I survey my audiences on why they stop doing business with one company in favor of another, it is very seldom because of price, and only slightly more often because of quality.

The overwhelming majority quit doing business with a company because of a bad personal experience. More specifically, because of the way someone treated them. This is not to say that price isn't important. In today's marketplace, price is as important than it's ever been, if not more so. But only as part of the whole package the customer calls *value,* which is the combination of price, quality, convenience, service, ownership experience, and every other factor in the buying decision.

You do not have to have the lowest price to compete successfully today, but you certainly have to demonstrate value. And you have to change the weight you give to the importance of the customer's total *experience* with your company. Of course, you don't throw out quality or price as important factors in the business equation, you promote them to the expected level. Service and experience have now emerged as the primary competitive factors. You must adjust accordingly.

What does that mean in terms of competition? To state the obvious, it means that the customer's experience of doing business with you has become the new competitive factor. And for most of us, that's good news. Because if you're reading this right now, chances are pretty good that you have much more influence and power over the quality of service in your company than you do over the quality of products or the price of those products. So, you've got the power. What are you doing with it?

Service Today—Better or Worse?

Here is my very favorite question to ask audiences: "Is service better than it's ever been, or worse than it's ever been? Think carefully." I never know what kind of response I'm going to get. Sometimes the audience will split right down the middle. Or it can go with a strong majority of votes in either direction. Usually, there is a majority favoring the answer that service is worse than it's ever been.

I follow up that question with this: "Are our *expectations* for service higher than they've ever been?" And that's when I usually get almost unanimous agreement. We all agree that our standards for service are higher than ever before. The implications of higher customer expectations are huge for your business. It's the number one competitive issue . . . how to meet those expectations.

What about this idea that service is worse than it's ever been? There's a good chance that you agree with that assessment of today's service. Well, let's talk about it. Do you ever miss the good old days of customer service? Let's go back in time to those golden days of yesteryear when service was wonderful and we all supposedly walked around with a glow of pure customer satisfaction on our faces.

What did the procedure used to be for returning a product? You had to prove that the product was defective in some way, fill out forms, most definitely produce a receipt, and jump through hoops to get the seller to even consider an exchange or refund. If the item had been bought through a catalog, then your situation was even worse. You still had to go through the standard gyrations, only do it by mail and telephone. It was a hassle, any way you looked at it.

Compare that process with the typical experience of today. I recently needed to return a couple of DVDs that I had purchased on the Internet. I went to the seller's Web site, was greeted by my highly personalized greetings page, and immediately went to the returns page. On this page, they listed all of my orders from the previous 30 days. I chose the most recent order and went to a listing of all the DVDs that were in that particular order. The page asked me to identify the DVDs I wanted to return, and then gave me a list of options to choose from as the reason I was returning them.

Here's where it got very, very cool indeed. After identifying the items I was returning, I was given the option of going to a page that I then printed on my printer.

This page was the preaddressed label to use when returning the items, including the postage. I didn't even have to go to the post office to buy postage. This experience is not particularly out of the ordinary today.

We are spoiled rotten. Think about service today and you'll have to agree that technology, policies, and processes have improved immensely over the "good old days."

BUT . . . And this is one whale of a big BUT . . . The only thing that matters in the real world of dealing with customers is that even in those examples in which service is better than it used to be—the customer still isn't happy! She wants more! While service standards have gotten better and better, our service expectations as customers have gotten higher and higher.

This isn't a problem—it's an opportunity! As long as the customer keeps raising the bar, you keep having the opportunity to beat the pants off your competitors who can't keep up the pace.

If you're good at what you do, you should be very thankful for customers who constantly demand more and more. Because a constantly rising standard of service weeds out your competitors who really aren't all that great, and makes room for you. The customer is giving you the chance to encourage your competitors to find another line of work.

The Customer Decides

You may as well make a conscious decision to let your customers make up the rules. They already do anyway. Many businesses are struggling with this new reality—that the customer is quite literally in charge of the game now, and that if you aren't willing to play by those rules, well, you can't play at all. They won't let you.

Let's look again at the car business. Survey after survey has shown that most people hate the process of buying a car. They love having a new car. But they hate the process of buying a car. Why? Because they feel like they are being manipulated by a car salesman who will do or say anything to make the sale. They feel like they are being bamboozled and that they have no control over the process.

But a few things have happened to change the rules of the game. Quality has improved across the board and the competitive focus has shifted to the customer's satisfaction with service, the buying process, and the total experience of buying and owning a car. Some car dealers and salespeople get it. Some don't.

My wife, Annette, wanted to trade her car for a late model used sport utility vehicle. At the first dealer we visited, the salesman was a caricature of the car buyer's nightmare. And he didn't have the slightest clue about just how inept he was. He was all fast talk, full of numbers and mileage, and "what will it take to put you in a new vehicle today?"

Finally, Annette gave me the word, "Let's get out of here." The poor goof of a salesman had no idea what he had done wrong. He truly needed to go to the bank, take some money out of his account, go somewhere, and buy a clue (and take his sales manager and the dealer with him). Salespeople like this are in the process of getting a wake up call from the marketplace.

Annette and I went to another dealer. We walked around the used car lot, looking over the sport utility vehicles. At one point, a salesman ambled out to us and said, "I just wanted to let you folks know I see you out here. I'm not ignoring you." I was reminded of what my friend Marty at K&T Lamp store taught me, that there's "a difference between being ignored and being left alone." The salesman continued, "If you find one you'd like to take for a spin, or if you have any questions, just give me a wave." We exchanged names, shook hands, and he ambled back inside to keep watch from the showroom. Cool.

How Do You Want to Buy a Car?

After a little more looking, Annette found one particular vehicle that she was interested in. We waved at the salesman, who came back out and said, "Who's buying a car today?" "I am." Annette replied. "Annette, how do you want to buy a car? By that I mean, there are lots of ways I can help you. I can tell you about each vehicle that you might be interested in, or I can stick with you and just answer questions if you have any, or if you want to take one for a drive, I can get you the keys. I'll be happy to ride with you, or you and Joe can take it by yourselves and just bring it back after you've had a good drive in it. What would suit you best?"

Annette said, "We'd like to take this one for a drive. And we'll just take it by ourselves." "Fine," the salesman said. "I'll check with you when you get back. Let me run get the keys for you." As we drove off the lot, Annette turned to me and said, "I don't know if he's going to sell me this one. But he's going to sell me something. I like him." He let her make up the rules. And she bought the car.

Not long after that, I was speaking to a convention of car dealers at a convention in Cancun, Mexico. I told them the story of Annette's experience. I said that for them to succeed in the new marketplace, they had to stop manipulating customers, and let the customer control the buying process.

This news was greeted by total silence. As my friend Dale Irvin would say, "They looked at me like a dog looks at a ceiling fan." They simply didn't understand what I was saying. Let the customer control the buying process? It was like I was speaking a foreign language. Just like they didn't understand why so many of their former customers were firing them and going to the new breed of auto dealers who treat people honestly, openly, and with respect.

Exceeding Expectations—Really?

I always cringe a little when I work with a company, and there are lots and lots of them, that says they will "Exceed the

Customer's Expectations." Fine. Wonderful. Now let me ask you a very important question. Do you have even a remote idea how incredibly high your customer's expectations are? With today's demanding customer you are going to have to do cartwheels, triple back flips, and swan dives through hoops of fire just to come close to even meeting their expectations, much less exceeding them. Now don't get me wrong. I agree that exceeding the customer's expectations is a very powerful thing to do. Just remember that *you* don't decide if you've exceeded the customer's expectations. The customer does.

No business today automatically has "customers for life." And that's a big change from the way things used to be. The customer's attitude today is this: "Whatever you're selling, I can find it somewhere else. I can find it just as good, for the same price or better." And they're probably right.

Some businesses, almost by nature, it seemed, were able to hold on to their customers without even really trying. Let's look at a business that is now incredibly competitive because of deregulation and, more importantly, changing customer attitudes. It's the customer's perception of himself and his own power that has done more to open up this business than anything else.

Who's in Control Now?

Let's talk about banking. Consider the following questions: Did your parents do business pretty much their whole adult lives, and maybe still do, with one bank? The vast majority of people answer yes. That's the way banking used to be. You opened a checking account, maybe a savings account, got a car loan, and boom—you were locked in. When your parents said they were going to the bank, you didn't have to ask which one. It was THE bank.

But look at how the world has changed. Do you do business with more than one bank? Again, almost everyone says yes. It's not at all unusual to do business today with more than one bank at a time.

Now here comes the really important question. Have you ever *fired* a bank? When I ask that question of audiences not only do most people raise their hands, they smile, giggle, or outright laugh at the same time their hands go up. They can't do it without kind of gloating about it a little bit. Why? Power. They've got it. And they like it.

Let me illustrate the way this particular seller/buyer–banker/customer relationship has changed. I'm a banker's kid. I grew up around bankers, and I do a great deal of work with banks today. Twenty or thirty years ago, if I went to the bank to try and get a car loan, who made up the rules? The banker, of course. And we both knew it.

The scene would go something like this: I go into my neighborhood bank to have a chat with my friendly neighborhood banker. Let's call him Jim. It's a friendly bank and Jim's a friendly guy, but it's still very much a bank. I'm only the customer, I know my place, and I'm more than a little intimidated.

So I walk up to Jim's desk and say, "Hi Jim, I wanted to talk to you . . . uh . . . can I sit down? . . . uh . . . Okay thanks. I wanted to talk to you about getting a lo, lo, loan . . . uh . . . my uh . . . my car is an old, old car and I've been, you know, seeing ads for all these new cars and I was thinking well okay, maybe not a new car but a better car. But even to get a better car I would need, from you, a lo, lo, well, you know, money. I need a loan, Jim. I need a loan." And Jim the friendly neighborhood banker says, "Well, Joe, we'll see. Fill out this three-page application form, turn it back in, I'll run it past the consumer loan committee. They're meeting in the morning, I think. I'll give you a call tomorrow."

The next day I'm at work. Jim calls and says, "Joe I've got some good news. Come on down to the bank." So I go to the bank and Jim says, "Joe, I've got some good news for you. We have decided to give you this loan. But just a couple of things to take care of. Now you do have a 25 percent down payment or trade in to put on this car, don't you?"

Do you remember that? Remember when you used to have to have some actual money to buy a car? Jim continues, "I noticed you wanted the loan for three years. I don't think so, Joe. I think we'd feel better with a two-year term on this. And we're going to charge you 31 percent interest." At this point I would squeal with glee, "I got the loan!!! Ohhh happy day! The bank has favored and honored me by deciding to do business with me!!! Oh, joy unbounded!!!" And that's the way it was then, it was the seller in control.

That Was Then—This Is Now

This is now. I walk into the bank, straight to the banker's desk. Take a seat, look Jim in the eye and say, "Hey. Car loans. Whatcha got? Talk to me. Cause I checked with a couple of other banks and checked with the credit union, and I know what the car companies have got on financing, so let's bottom line this thing." Jim, the friendly neighborhood banker, eagerly and anxiously says, "Oh, wait, we've got good loans. You don't have to go anywhere else! And it won't take any time at all. Just fill out this. . . . I'll tell you what, just sign this index card. Just sign it, let me run it past my branch manager. She'll be back in just a few minutes, I'm sure. I'll tell you what, why don't you go back to work. You give me an hour, I'll give you a call and we'll put you in a new car."

You tell today's customer that and what's their response going to be? "An hour!!! To do what? I mean, hey, I'm on my lunch hour man, I kinda wanted to get a new car and take it back to work you know?!! What's this on you desk? Hello, excuse me, is this a computer? You call up my name, see my record, do what you have to do and give me the money or not! I don't think so, babe, I don't think so."

And the customer walks out, gets into the car, and drives down the street thinking, "What was that ad I heard on the radio this morning going to work? Some ad for the ACME Bank. Yeah, the ACME Bank, the '20 Minute Yes.' What's that all about? Why here's an ACME Bank, now."

The customer walks in and says, "Excuse me, ACME Banker. '20 Minute Yes.' What's that all about?" And the ACME Banker says, "20 Minute Yes? You must be getting a new car! Get a red one! Get a fast one! Have some fun! Have some coffee! I'll go get the money!"

Firing the Bank

Guess what? Jim the banker's customer has a new best friend and Jim the banker's bank has just been fired. By the way, I often will ask an audience if they could have fired the banker 20 years ago. The response I get always amazes me and it's very revealing about how we perceived our role as customer back then. The vast majority of people will say "No. I couldn't fire the banker 20 years ago."

Are you kidding? Of course you could. Twenty years ago. Thirty years ago. Fifty years ago! You could walk up to the bank manager and say "Close my accounts. I'm not happy. You're fired." And they would have to do it. But it was so ingrained in us that we were *just the customer*. We perceived ourselves as having no power whatsoever.

And it's not just banks we're talking about here. You name the business. The rules are the same. Some businesses that used to have customers for life now see customer turnover like they never could have imagined. The most obvious example is probably in telecommunications. It's become rare to find someone who hasn't changed long distance companies at least once, if not many times. I am always amazed at the growing numbers of people in my audiences who say that in the past three years they have fired a doctor for "having a bad attitude." What people are realizing is this, the doctor works for them, not the other way around. You give today's customers what they want, the way they want it, when they want it. If you don't, the customer walks, and she'll do it in a New York minute.

Benchmark the World

I look at my business and I think I'm special. You look at your business and probably think you're special. But guess what? Our customers and prospects don't think we're so special. They see sameness. They think, rightly or wrongly, that they can get the same thing somewhere else. Until we understand that reality, and take the steps necessary to truly differentiate ourselves from the competition, we are constantly at risk of losing our customers.

It seems like every company loves to benchmark. They compare themselves to the other companies who do what they do. And, if they are at least as good as the other companies who do what they do, or most certainly if they are better, they believe that the windows of prosperity will open up and riches and joy and all things good and wonderful will pour down upon them forevermore. And because they are as good as or better than the companies that do what they do, their customers will be happy with them and the world will be at peace.

Benchmarking those companies that do pretty much the same thing that you do is fine, for as far as it goes. But it doesn't go nearly far enough. You've got to do more.

You've got to look beyond your particular industry.

Your Competition Is Everybody

The problem is that we often fall into the trap of comparing our performance to that of the other companies who make what we make, do what we do, sell what we sell. But our customers have no such neat categories. Our customers compare us to Federal Express who delivers on time and the car dealer's service department that sent them a thank you note, and the dry cleaner where every employee knows them by name.

We all got caught up in the great benchmarking frenzy. Be better than everybody else that does what you do!! And you will triumph!!! If only it were that simple. The real world of customers doesn't work that way. You, like me, get compared to *everybody* that your customers do business with.

I first got the great "Aha!" that I was actually competing against everybody else out there, regardless of the business they are in, in 1983. My client was a chain of retail stores. In a speech one day to the troops, the president of the company, almost in an off-hand way, made this observation: "You know, we've got to be as dependable as the light switch on the wall. We've got to be as friendly as the corner market. And our service has to be as good as anyone's out there, regardless of the business they're in. We have to be the best experience our customers have."

If somebody out there provides the level of service I want, then I want my provider of everything else to give me that same level of service. Never mind that they are in completely different businesses. It doesn't matter. Today's customer doesn't care.

Pizza Guy: 1—Banker: 0

I was giving a speech on customer service to the Young President's Organization in Toledo, Ohio, when a member of the audience, the president of a manufacturing company, shared a powerful story with the group. Let's call him Tony. He told us of a recent experience that had caused him to reevaluate the level of service he was receiving from all of his vendors, as well as the level of service he was providing to his customers.

It was all prompted by a call one night from the pizza guy. That's right. The pizza guy. It seems that this manufacturing mogul orders a pizza from his local pizza place about once every two weeks. They deliver it. He eats it. He likes it. Every two weeks.

Recently, he had been out of the country for almost a month on a business trip. His second night back home he got a call from the pizza place. "Hello, this is Bob, the manager down at the pizza place. We just wanted to know, how was that last pizza we delivered to you a few weeks ago? Was everything okay?" "Well," said Tony, "Yes, it was fine. Why do you ask?" "Well," said Bob, "You usually order a pizza from us every couple of weeks, and we noticed that it's been over a month since you've called, and we were just wanting to be sure that everything was okay with that last pizza. Because if you weren't satisfied with it for any reason, we wanted to find out what was wrong and make it right." "No, there's no problem at all," said Tony. "I've just been out of town for a while." Bob says, "Well, that's a relief, sir. Glad you're back in town. Give us a call when you want a pizza."

Tony thinks about this experience for a while and after about 15 minutes, he's hungry for a pizza so he calls the pizza place back and orders one. But there's a bigger lesson to be learned here.

Tony told us that the next day he called his commercial banker, and when the banker said "Hi, Tony. What can I do for you?" Tony said to him, "Well, I learned something last night." "Oh, yes?" says the banker, "What's that?" "Well," says Tony, "I learned that my business is more important to the pizza guy than it is to you." Strong stuff.

Tony said that he was now in the process of using the pizza guy's level of interest, attention, and communication as the standard of performance in his own business with vendors, employees, and customers. The new reality is that you have to meet a whole set of customer expectations that have nothing to do with the business you're in. It has to do with the business that somebody else is in. Somewhere out there today one of your customers is dealing with someone who is raising the service bar. And the next time that customer comes to you, guess what? You've got to meet that new level or pay the price in dissatisfaction or a lost customer.

You can't look at your business anymore the way you've always looked at it because the customer couldn't care less how you look at it. You've got to look at your business the way your customer looks at it. It really doesn't matter how well you think you're doing. All that matters is how well the customer thinks you're doing.

Your customer wants to know if you can do it as well as the insurance company, the bookstore on the Internet, and the pizza guy down the street. Whoever does it great—that's your standard.

Case Study— Tractor Supply Company

A Raving Fan

When I am asked to give an example of a Category of One company, Tractor Supply Company always comes to mind. I've worked as a consultant for Tractor Supply off and on for 20 years. I've worked with hundreds of really great companies over the years, but none has impressed me more than Tractor Supply.

In 1938, Charles E. Schmidt Sr. of Chicago, Illinois, established a mail order tractor parts business. In 1939, it had grown into a successful retail store in Minot, North Dakota. Today, Tractor Supply Company is one of the largest retail chains in America. It serves full- and part-time farmers and rancher, hobby farmers, rural homeowners, and contractors, operating over 420 stores in 30 states.

There is no measure of success by which they do not succeed. Their growth has been steady. Their annual revenues
are well over a billion dollars. My admiration for the way they
have achieved their success is unbounded. I am a raving fan of
this company and I think it stands as a model for anyone who
wants to make their organization a Category of One.

It's ultimately the customer who decides if you're truly a
Category of One company. I could quite literally fill this
book with nothing but letters from satisfied Tractor Supply
customers. Let me illustrate with three small examples of
the kind of connection that Tractor Supply makes with its
customers.

Just to Be around Them

The following comments were taken from customers' letters
to Tractor Supply Company:

> I have been in your store several times and the employees al-
> ways seem to make you feel at home and relaxed while you
> are shopping. They will ask if they can assist you in finding
> something. If not, then they leave you alone to go at your
> own pace. They are very helpful in finding what you need
> and making suggestions that may help you. At the checkout
> counter, they are very friendly and make you feel like you
> want to buy something else just to be around them.

> In this world of automation and computers, it is so re-
> freshing to find such caring and beautiful people.

> Thank you for everything. God bless you all. Keep up your
> great work.

You might want to go back and read these simple yet powerful expressions of customer satisfaction and loyalty. Look at the words they use. It's not just about "finding the right product" or "having a great price." Those are commodity factors.

Tractor Supply's customers use words like "caring and beautiful people" and "God bless you all."

And if that weren't inspiring enough, how about the inspiration of they "make you feel like you want to buy something else just to be around them." We're definitely on to something when customers stay and buy stuff just so they can hang out with you!

Transcend Commodity and Defy Comparison

Tractor Supply sells supplies to the part-time and hobby farmer. Their customers tend to work in town but live in an outlying area on a small farm of 5 to 10 acres. They might have a couple of horses and some other animals, and they are in love with the rural lifestyle. This is Tractor Supply's market niche.

Tractor Supply Company is positioned somewhere in the mix of big-box retailers like Wal-Mart and Home Depot, farmer's co-ops, and hardware stores. But they've managed to create their own category. No other kind of store carries the product mix that Tractor Supply has. And not many organizations of any kind have the mix of leadership and values that Tractor Supply has.

The product mix could be copied. Their prices could be matched or even beat. But the unique Tractor Supply Company culture is the strength that enables them to transcend commodity and defy comparison.

Legendary Service

The Tractor Supply Company mission is powerful in its clarity and simplicity: "To work hard, have fun, and make money by providing legendary service and great products at everyday low prices." Okay. We're going to work hard, have fun, and make money. Fair enough. There's no part of that that I don't understand. Unless all three of these things are happening at once, we're not fulfilling our mission. Great products and everyday low prices take care of competing at a commodity level. And certainly service has to be a part of the plan.

But "legendary" service? Now we're getting into something that is impossible to quantify and open to interpretation. But it's words like "legendary" that Tractor Supply isn't afraid to use and it's what powers the organization to create legendary customer satisfaction and loyalty. Remember, some Tractor Supply customers want to buy something else just to be around them. I'd say that qualifies as "legendary."

The Foundation

The foundation on which Tractor Supply has built its success can be found in their 10 values that are posted everywhere throughout the company, carried in the pocket of every employee, and talked about all the time.

1. *Ethics:* Do the "right thing" and always encourage others to do the right, honest, and ethical things.

2. *Respect:* Treat others with the same personal and professional consideration we expect for ourselves.
3. *Balance:* Manage your time for both business and personal success.
4. *Winning attitude:* Have a "can-do" attitude. Be positive, upbeat, and focused. We are winners!
5. *Communication:* Share information, ask questions, listen effectively, speak thoughtfully, and let ideas live.
6. *Development:* Learn from each other. Teach, coach, and listen. Create an environment where everyone can be a "star."
7. *Teamwork:* Value different viewpoints. Execute the agreed-upon plans. Together, everyone achieves more!
8. *Change:* Accept it. Embrace it. Initiate it. Do everything better, faster, and cheaper.
9. *Initiative:* Seek opportunities. Use good judgment. Take intelligent risks. Champion ideas.
10. *Accountability:* Know your responsibilities. Live up to your commitments.

Most companies have a good set of values and Tractor Supply's aren't necessarily unique. What is unique is that their values don't sit in desk drawers to be taken out at the annual meeting and read with great ceremony then be put away at the end of the meeting. At Tractor Supply, their values are the rules of the road for how they do everything, every day, all day long. They are talked about constantly. You simply cannot be around the Tractor Supply organization, much less work for it, without seeing the impact of these values on how they run their business.

What Leadership Looks Like

Joe Scarlett is the chairman of the board and chief executive officer of Tractor Supply, and in the 20 years that I've watched him work, he has come to define leadership for me. My favorite definition of leadership is that a leader constantly reminds us who we are. Everyone at Tractor Supply Company has a clear knowledge of who they are and what's important, and this is their great strength.

I interviewed Joe to get some insight into his views on leadership:

Calloway: What differentiates Tractor Supply Company from the competition?

Scarlett: There are a number of things that differentiate us. One strong point is our culture. We've carved out this mission and values statement that we really live and really practice. When you compare us to other similar employers, they tend very often to have a very loose and undefined culture. In our company, you can talk to almost anybody and they'll be able to recite back our mission because it's there and they hear it all the time.

Calloway: You talk about "living the mission statement." How do you pull that off? What's the secret to making a mission statement "real" instead of just something that you read at the company meetings once a year?

Scarlett: Twice a year, we have our big companywide meetings. And at every one of those meetings over the years, they hear me talking about "work hard, have fun, make money, take care of the customer," and so on. And I talk about it nonstop. Whenever they see me coming, they know I'm going to talk about it.

For years, at an elevating pace, more of our people are doing the same thing. We just finished our summer meetings. I show up on the last day to talk about the mission, and unbeknownst to me, on the first day of the meeting, the district managers have already done the same thing. More and more people are taking ownership of it. It is in our publication. The column I write for the company magazine is always tied in one way or another to our mission. I can't tell you how, other than we talk about it all the time. And everybody's really taking a sense of ownership. They've heard it for so long and so repetitively that everyone buys into it and it becomes a way of life.

Every quarter we have a meeting here at the store support center. We introduce everyone who's new to the company at the beginning of that meeting. At the end of the meeting, I tell all those new people to stick around. For half an hour, I talk with every new employee about our mission and our values and I welcome them to the company that way.

In our stores, when someone starts working for us there's an introductory video with me and Jim Wright, our president, talking about the mission and the values. It's just everywhere. I don't think there's any real secret to it other than just being repetitive. Some companies just plaster their mission up on the walls and let it sit there. We keep talking about it all the time. It's got a life of its own.

Calloway: Is talking about mission and values all the time the key to leadership?

Scarlett: Yes. I guess you could put it that way. We are consistent about what we're doing.

We say the same thing over and over again and we focus on the same issues. I think there's a sense of leadership because we're consistently talking about working hard, having fun, making money, taking care of the customer. We talk about the same thing over and over again so we're always going in the same direction.

It's interesting that when we hire people from other companies, a couple of the things that they always say are that they like our business and our niche and our customers. But they also like the fact that we don't change direction every day. So many companies are going one way one month and another way the next month and they are always chasing the latest fad. We don't go for the latest fad. We stay consistently doing the same thing over and over again. They love that. They also like the fact that we've got a strong set of values and there's never any compromising. Ethics is ethics and you either do it the right way or you go somewhere else. In other companies sometimes they might see some bending of the rules and they get confused by that.

Every year we have a discussion here about what should the theme of the manager's meeting be. The people planning the meeting get excited and say, "Oh yeah, we've got to have a theme! Every meeting has to have a theme!" And I keep saying okay, but whatever it is let's not make too big a deal out of it because the theme is really the same every year. We're going to talk about our mission and our values.

Mission and Value Driver

To give you an idea of what this kind of "know who we are" leadership looks like here is a letter that Joe sent to every Tractor Supply Company employee:

June 27, 2002

Dear Team Member:

"America's Corporate Meltdown" is the headline in this morning's *USA Today*. The article covers the wrong doing at WorldCom, Enron, Rite Aid, and so on with the implication that American business leaders are unethical and dishonest. This, obviously, casts a black cloud over all of us in the business community.

I am firmly convinced that only a tiny fraction of American business leaders are not honest and ethical. It is truly a shame that a few greedy bums are casting such a dark shadow over all of us. I, for one, am mad! I hope these criminals are fairly tried and spend a long time behind bars.

At Tractor Supply, we are a mission- and value-driven company. "We talk the talk and we walk the walk." Our number one value is Ethics—"Do the right thing and always encourage others to do the right, honest and ethical things." It is our pledge to you that Tractor Supply will always "Walk the high road"—always strive to make the most ethical business decisions.

The stories about people losing their life savings in 401(k) plans that were not managed correctly are truly heart wrenching. At Tractor Supply Company, you personally direct the investment of all of your 401(k) money and the management of these plans is by a third party. Markets go up and markets go down, but in the long term those of you who have Tractor Supply 401(k) programs should be building a solid base of retirement funds for your future.

Again, I reiterate that our number one value is Ethics. We teach the right thing, we do the right thing, and we will be forever committed to the highest ethical standards.

Regardless of the current headlines, American business leaders are the best in the world. I urge you not to let the misdeeds of a limited number of people at a limited number of companies erode your confidence in our business leaders.

Sincerely,

Joe Scarlett
Head Coach

When I asked Joe Scarlett about the importance of ethics at Tractor Supply Company, he said, "We don't tolerate any shenanigans. We expect everyone to do the right, honest, and ethical things all the time and we just don't tolerate anything less. I talk about it in the management training classes. I say if there's ever any question in your mind about ethics, just stop and call your district or regional manager, call the HR department, call the president of the company, call me. Don't do anything crazy and don't ever get tempted to do anything other than the right thing. Because in the long run if you get sideways ethically with us you're just not going to be here."

Whatever It Takes

A key to Tractor Supply Company's legendary customer service and the resulting legendary customer satisfaction and loyalty is its policy on doing whatever it takes to make the customer happy. This policy applies to every Tractor Supply employee. Talk about rolling the empowerment dice! Here's a letter from Joe Scarlett to all employees as printed on the first page of the company newsletter, *The Voice:*

> You Are Empowered. Everybody—go look at the sign over the checkout—it says:
>
> ## SATISFACTION GUARANTEED
>
> All team members have the authority
> to do whatever it takes.
>
> Precisely translated, this means that we trust you to take care of customers no matter what the circumstances. You are empowered!
>
> I read every customer comment and take great pride in sending complimentary notes back to individuals and stores. We are all so very proud of you when your customers go out of their way to give you a "pat on the back."
>
> We also get comments that are not so positive. Compliments are our biggest category of customer comments, but here are the next three most common categories of customer comments:
>
> - Product issues: These are comments about products that don't fit the customer's needs correctly and products that are somehow defective. You can resolve every one of these issues at the store. As soon as you find that a customer has a problem, the official words to use to the customer are "What would you like me to do about that?" Then, simply do what the customer wants—you can't go wrong. We trust you; you

are empowered to take care of the problem. You have total support form every supplier and total support from Tractor Supply Company.

- *Chckout speed:* We have a simple policy called "Three's a Crowd." As soon as there are more than three customers in line, our cashier is empowered to get on the public address system and get the second register open. If both registers are open, it's time to get one more person up front to help expedite the checkout process. We operate relatively small stores in which customers can park close to the door and receive quick service. You are empowered to make sure that customers really get checked out quickly—it's a major part of our success formula.
- *Attitude:* I cringe every time I see a comment about poor attitude. This is totally within your control and there is simply no excuse for the display of a bad attitude. We have a great spirit in our company, a clear mission, a strong set of values, and clearly expect every single member of our team to have a positive attitude. If you don't have a positive attitude, Tractor Supply is not the place for you to work.

To be very clear, we simply do not want to get comments about product, checkout speed, or attitude. Every one of these topics is completely within your control. We trust you and you are empowered!

When you resolve a customer issue at the store, you win. When a customer issue is resolved in Nashville (company headquarters), the issues may be resolved but the customer will never feel quite the same about you and your store. So again take care of all issues at the store.

The "Shopping Experience" you provide will determine customer loyalty in your store. There is no task more important than taking care of your customers.

Your goal must be to help me receive nothing but positive customer comments—that is a big win for both of us. Remember, you are the master—you are empowered to "Do Whatever It Takes." We trust you!

Little Things—Big Results

At Tractor Supply Company, they stay focused. They know what drives sales and creates customer loyalty and so they reinforce those factors all the time, year after year. As the chairman and CEO, Joe Scarlett takes care of the big picture by helping team members stay focused on what works. Here's another example of part of Joe's column from the Tractor Supply Company employee newsletter:

> We are a sales driven company. Our vision is for Tractor Supply Company to provide the very best customer service in the farm and ranch store business.
>
> We love our customers. We do whatever it takes. We win because we have great people with great attitudes. We win because we really do provide the best customer service in the farm and ranch store business.
>
> Here are two challenges for every one of you:
>
> 1. Learn Your Customer's Names—There is nothing more compelling than saying "Good Morning, Mr. Jones" and "Good Afternoon, Mrs. Anderson." When you greet by name, customers will always choose your store first—that is a real competitive advantage. Greeting customers by name is your most powerful selling tool. I challenge you to learn one customer's name per

week—50 customers' names in a year. You are challenged to learn your customer's names!

2. Walk Customers to the Product—Don't point, don't direct, just simply walk the customer to the product. Now you have the opportunity to explain the features and benefits of the product and to make sure the customer gets all the related items to complete the project. You also have the opportunity to probe about additional sales opportunities. If you are not familiar with the product, get the customer started and then go find some help. You are challenged to always walk the customer to the product!

No Ivory Tower

It's pretty rare to find a chairman and CEO of a company who deals with things such as encouraging employees to call customers by name and to walk customers to the product. It's even more rare to find a chairman and chief executive officer who talks about these same things over and over year after year. And it's exceedingly rare to find a company with the performance of Tractor Supply Company. Makes you believe that maybe it isn't rocket science after all, doesn't it?

Joe Scarlett and Jim Wright, president and chief operating officer, have offices in TSC headquarters in Nashville, Tennessee. But it's not even called headquarters. It's the Store Support Center. At Tractor Supply, they choose their words very carefully.

And at Tractor Supply, the leadership doesn't sit in an ivory tower. You'll find them in the trenches with the team members, constantly reminding everyone of who they are and what's important here.

Eye on the Ball

Lest you think that Tractor Supply is one big feel-good, let's all hold hands and recite the company values lovefest, let me assure you that this is one very savvy group of business operators. Jim Wright keeps everyone's eye on the ball all the time and makes the organization run as it's designed to run.

Jim came to Tractor Supply from Tire Kingdom, a Florida-based chain of retail tire stores, where he was president and chief operating officer. Jim's expertise at inventory control is a key to the success of Tractor Supply. And his leadership in operations keeps everyone razor sharp on the execution of the details of the business.

A Great Place to Work

Jim and the rest of the Tractor Supply leadership team are dedicated to making Tractor Supply an employer of choice for the best people in retail. Jim talked about this in the company newsletter:

> I am struck by the awesome size of the responsibility we all face to make Tractor Supply *a great place to work*. It is imperative that we become the employer of choice in our category; for only then can we become the store of choice for our customers.
>
> Each of us brings a unique set of life experience and learning to our company. Each of us is also a work in progress. Each of us will drop the ball occasionally.

However, if each of us is committed to the balls dropped by others and if each of us is committed to learning from one another and teaching one another, we indeed become *a great place to work*. Then we'll become *a great place to shop*. Then we will, as a result, become *a great place to invest*.

A Great Brand

I believe that Jim Wright is a Category of One president and COO, because he understands that operations isn't about systems and processes as much as it is about the people who operate those systems and processes. Tractor Supply invests in awesome technology, but they never get their priorities mixed up. It's a people business, not just in a slogan, but in their day-to-day operations. This focus on people is the foundation of the Tractor Supply brand.

Jim puts it this way, "The brand of a company has been best described as: 'Everything over, under, and around the company.' Each of us impacts the value of our brand in everything we do. A short, efficient checkout line is a positive to the brand; a long, slow line is a negative. Merchandise that performs as or better than expected is a positive; less than expected performance detracts from the brand. Helping a customer load out whenever possible builds the brand; not going the extra step detracts from the brand."

Becoming the Brand of Choice

Blake Fohl is the vice president of marketing and advertising for Tractor Supply. To gain some insight into how a Category of One company becomes the brand of choice, I sat down with Blake to talk about the Tractor Supply brand and what it really means:

Calloway: I've been working with Tractor Supply and going to your managers' meetings for almost 20 years. You invest an extraordinary amount of time and energy in training and motivation.

Fohl: We believe that there is a retail engine, and the engine begins with having well-trained, well-motivated, well-led team members. That is the first thing that you have to have. Once you have that people engine started within your company, that will transfer to the customer, and then you will have happy customers. And when you have well-motivated, well-trained, well-led team members and happy customers, you have sales, which create happy investors. That leads to accomplishing our strategic goal to be the best place to work, the best place to shop, and the best place to invest.

Calloway: What about those people who would say that all the things you do at your meetings are corny. That it's just a bunch of cheerleading and rah-rah motivational stuff that's just for show.

Fohl: I guess there'll always be jaded people. Not everybody likes to party like everybody else. It's part of our culture. And if you can't see the personal pride, the passion that goes on at those meetings, then you're not really looking. All I would say is look in their faces. Forget the noise. Forget the banners. Forget all of that. Just look in the eyes of the faces of the men and women that are there. That will tell you that there's something here deep.

Calloway: How important is the concept of branding at Tractor Supply?

Fohl: Between those engines—the engines of creating the happy team member, the happy customer, and the happy investor, is this thing called *branding*. In our viewpoint, this is how we look at branding. If you ask, "What is a brand?"—and at Tractor Supply the goal is not to be a house of brands but to be a branded house. That is a point of differentiation. In our viewpoint, a brand is the essence of who you are, your reason for being, and how you emotionally relate to your customers.

Calloway: What does "brand" mean at Tractor Supply?

Fohl: Let's dissect what a brand is. It's your essence. It's your culture. So what is our culture at TSC? Every person in the company, every office, every cubicle has our mission, vision, and values—and it's not just something that's printed. If you take the 10 values that we live, this is our road map for how we interact with each other, and how we interact with our customers. So this, in essence, becomes our culture. Joe Scarlett becomes our cultural leader. He believes this; he's passionate about this. This is the consistency. This is what we talk about at every meeting, no matter how routine the meeting might be. Everything relates back to the culture. The culture is one piece of the brand.

Calloway: What are some of the other aspects of branding for your team?

Fohl: Branding is our reason for being. The reason for us to be is that we're going to work hard, have fun, and make money, while providing legendary service and great products at everyday prices. Now we have 50 percent of the Tractor Supply Company brand—our culture, our reason for being. So what is the emotional connection that we make with our customers?

We are a niche business. If you look at our customer segmentation, they all have something in common, and that's what makes us unique. They all have a desire for a particular lifestyle. We help enable that lifestyle. We enable that lifestyle through an eclectic collection of products. When I go out and talk about Tractor Supply, I say that you can find everything in our store somewhere else, but you can't go anywhere else and find everything in our store. It's this unique, eclectic collection of products that enables people with a common lifestyle, a rural lifestyle, to have fulfillment and enjoyment of that lifestyle, and to live life on their own terms.

Calloway: So is your brand largely about helping your customers create a particular lifestyle?

Fohl: Our customers are people who are willing to make that commitment of driving from outside the city into work every day and back out again every day so that they can live a lifestyle out of town. It's so much more than a hobby. In America, you have fads, which can turn into trends, which can turn into hobbies, which then can turn into lifestyles. As a brand, you want to be serving a lifestyle. You can't have a sustainable brand around a fad. Our emotional connection with our customers is built around that lifestyle.

Calloway: What about price as a part of the brand? How important is pricing as a differentiator?

Fohl: We want to remove price as an obstacle to shopping. We just don't want it to be an issue. We want to build the trust that we're going to have fair, everyday low prices.

Calloway: How important is the Tractor Supply culture in building the brand? Is it more important than the products?

Fohl: Our approach to branding is that we want to leverage our culture through the brand. It's the culture that makes the difference. In our mind, the Tractor Supply brand creates a competitive advantage that differentiates us from the competition and provides sustainable market share value. And it's a competitive advantage that's not easily duplicated or replicated. Anybody could go put a store in and fill it up with the same products that we carry. But they don't have our culture and it's our culture—the thousands of men and women who work here—that are the touch points of the brand. They are the ones who touch our millions of customers and our potential customers.

Calloway: Strong leadership has been a key to the success of Tractor Supply, hasn't it?

Fohl: Great companies with great brands start with an entrepreneurial spirit and a great leader. What did Herb Kelleher do at Southwest Airlines? What did Sam Walton do at Wal-Mart? To protect the sustainability, you have to leverage the culture. Joe Scarlett fostered and helped grow the culture, but if we do this thing right and if we live this culture every day, the culture becomes bigger than Joe. It becomes a self-sustaining prophecy. And Joe, in his wisdom, has brought in people with the same passion and the same fire in the belly for this brand. By taking this brand and starting with every man and woman in this company, from the part-time people on up to the leadership, and by making them cultural brand advocates, it carries Joe's work on into the future. Jim Wright has it, and I've got it. It's his legacy, but it's the responsibility of all of us here to continue that legacy.

Calloway: What's the key to selling the brand internally at Tractor Supply?

Fohl: The fact of the matter is that it has to start in here, in this headquarters building, with Joe Scarlett. It has to be led by the senior management. It has to filter down to every associate in this headquarters and then go out to every one of the thousands of people that work for us.

    What we're trying to do is let Susie the cash register operator understand how living our values and living our culture increases brand value for Tractor Supply and how it increases value for her. The mere fact that Susie at the cash register takes the time to learn one to two customer's names each week so that when they walk through the door she can say "Hey, Bill, how are you doing? How are your kids?"—that's the power of our culture. Where in America can you go today where people know your name or even care who you are? That simple act, which is reflected in our values, is a touch point to the brand. Susie is adding value to the Tractor Supply brand in that simple act of remembering a customer's name.

Calloway: What about the employees who don't have customer contact? How do they add value to the brand?

Fohl: How does the employee in the back room who rarely sees a customer add value? He has ethics, he has teamwork, and he takes the initiative in seeing that the inventories are right so that the replenishment systems can work so that when we say that we are the most dependable supplier, that we have the inventory on the shelves—when he does a great job he is living the culture. He is fulfilling the brand promise of dependability and consistency.

Calloway: Is branding really about relationships and emotionally connecting with customers?

Fohl: It's all got to start with the thousands of employees that
are the brand touch points. When they are happy and well
trained, they become brand advocates. That carries over and
you create millions of customers who are brand believers. You
make an emotional connection with those customers who say,
"These people understand my lifestyle. They took the time
and the energy to go out and find the right products for me.
And along with those products they have the seasoned advice
that can help me live my lifestyle to the fullest."

Our people become brand stewards when they help our
customers so that they can enjoy that lifestyle. Our customers don't just shop with us because we've got the stuff
that they want. They know that Tractor Supply is there to
support their lifestyle. What a powerful engine it is to have
all those customers out there as brand believers. From that
you create real bottom line brand value.

Calloway: So you believe that the brand becomes a real differentiator for you.

Fohl: Brand does create a point of differentiation. That's why
we believe so strongly in the power of the Tractor Supply
brand. We don't shout and scream "Hey, we're branding!"
We quietly go about building the infrastructure and the
teams from the inside out.

Calloway: One of your key differentiators has to be the incredible and consistent level of enthusiasm in your managers
and employees. Your meetings are very motivational events.
But how do you sustain that enthusiasm and motivation between meetings?

Fohl: It's not easily done. Everything goes back to our values. One of our values is a winning attitude. Have a can-do, take-no-prisoners, winning attitude. That is done at the most basic level of the company. It's part of what makes America great. In this society, we all want to be winners and we have very motivated people that want to do better than their teammate in another store. We have stores competing against each other, we have districts competing against each other, and we've got regions competing against regions. This is a homebred process through voice mail, through e-mail—with every event that's going on there's always a challenge. There's always a challenge to stand up and say, "I can do better than you. Let me stand up and show you what I'm gonna do."

Calloway: The TSC culture is very real. It almost seems to be in the air no matter where you go in the company. And even though there's a great deal of competition within the company, it seems like everyone is pulling for everyone else to succeed.

Fohl: We immerse people in the Tractor Supply culture and it's contagious. It's absolutely contagious. You hear Joe Scarlett talk about our success stories. That's one way we keep this level of excitement and commitment. Everybody wants to be one of the success stories. They love to come up with an idea that the other stores or regions use to become more successful. There are people sending ideas to each other through e-mails and voice mails all over the company. Through the environment, the training, and the leadership it all becomes absolutely contagious. It's consistency. It's a way of life. It's our culture. It's what we do day in and day out.

Calloway: Your people really do seem to be happy for each other's success.

Fohl: It's like being in the Superbowl. And when the game is over, the losing team is hugging the guys that won and saying, "You know, only the best got here, and the best of the best won." There really is a passion and pride in our people and there's respect for each other. If the other team wins everyone recognizes that it's because they deserved to win. The thinking is if you can produce the results to get ahead of me you must have done something really special.

Calloway: You recently took on a lot of new managers through an acquisition. What was the challenge and opportunity of bringing in so many new people at once into the TSC culture?

Fohl: Number one, what made this such an incredible opportunity, and at the same time such an incredible challenge, was to take your direct competition, the people you'd been battling for years, who thought that they knew the right thing and you didn't, bring them into your company, and say, "Guys this is who we are and this is what we're about. We want to welcome you and we want to respect you for what you've done in the past. You're not burdened with what happened to your company. It was not you that caused what happened to your company. We want to bring you into our family, and it's all about our culture."

One of our values is respect and we showed them an enormous amount of respect. I don't know how many companies would ever do this, but when they came in we vested each associate with their 401(k) plan, their insurance, and their vacation. They were vested from day one, as if they had spent that number of years that they were with the other company with us. We sent them a real strong message. We wanted them to play ball our way, and our way is all about respect. We gave them the things that instantly made them a part of the team.

Calloway: You worked really hard to make them feel like equal team members from the very start, didn't you?

Fohl: We brought them in here we wrapped our arms around them and spent a lot of time talking to them real seriously about who we are, what we are, and how we do business. It's such a wholesome way of doing things that you'd have to be a very jaded person to not buy into believing that "Wow, these are great words, now can they live up to it." Well, we started living up to it before they came in the door. And we are upfront and honest about our expectations.

We talk to them about initiative, and about how we want their ideas and their concepts. With the new people that we got through the acquisition, we asked them all what worked for them and what was successful. What could we learn from them?

Calloway: You've got a policy that empowers any team member to do whatever it takes to make a customer happy.

Fohl: Empowerment—it's right above the door in every store: "Every associate is empowered to do whatever it takes."

Calloway: Do customers ever take an unfair advantage of that?

Fohl: Doesn't it make sense not to put policies in place that protect you from 1 percent of the people but that irritates 99 percent? As far as customers, sure there might be a few people that would take advantage of us and our policies.

But for every one that takes advantage of us, there are going to be 99 people that are wowed and amazed and whose levels of expectation were wildly exceeded, people who came in and said, "Man, I'm not believing this!" about our service. Now, I've got customer advocates. These people are going out and telling their neighbors, "What an experience!"

Calloway: Give me an example of the "whatever it takes" policy in action.

Fohl: I've got a guy doing tile work for me at my home who said, "Blake, I need a lawn mower. I want one of those big commercial type mowers." I said great, go down to TSC. He spent a thousand bucks on a big mower. He used it one time and came to me and said, "Blake, I am so embarrassed. This really isn't the kind of mower I need." I said no problem—take it back. Just take it back and watch what happens.

He took it back, and the store manager said, "Look, we just want you to be happy and be sure that you've got what you really want and need. Tell me about your property and let's figure out what will suit you best." The guy ends up getting an even more expensive lawn mower, but the real story is that he was just amazed. He said, "Blake, they took it back even though I had already used it and there was absolutely nothing wrong with it and I ended up getting something that I really love to use."

Now, we could have taken that same customer and said, "Sir, if there's nothing functionally wrong with the lawn mower, I'm sorry, but there's nothing we can do."

But that's not what it's all about with us.

What They Are All About

I think the thing that is most important in making Tractor Supply Company a Category of One company is that they know exactly what they are all about. They are all about working hard and having fun. They are all about doing whatever it takes to make the customer happy. They are all about doing the right thing, celebrating their victories, and having a winning attitude.

All of this might sound sugarcoated to some, and unrealistic in the tough, competitive world of business. But you only have to look at Tractor Supply's results to see that what they do is ultimately very pragmatic and profitable. They are a great example of what a business can be when you combine steady, unwavering leadership with good people who care about each other and the customers they serve. Add good products, competitive pricing, attention to detail, and the ability to execute the business plan consistently well every day, and you've created a Category of One.

The Heart of a Category of One Performer

Principles into Practice

To get to the heart of what makes a person or a company a Category of One performer, I talked with people who have put the principles into practice. They range from executives with very large companies to a dentist with a small but extraordinary and innovative practice. These are individuals that I admire personally, as well as professionally. I have learned much from each of them. I think you will, too. In Chapter 8, we focused on one of these companies, Tractor Supply Company. In this chapter, we will tell you about some others.

Raising a Ruckus

Studio Productions, as the company was known for over 20 years, began creating commercials and documentaries for a regional market in 1978. They were the production company behind the incredibly successful series of "Ernest" commercials, producing over 4,000 commercials, which were syndicated nationwide. Studio Productions branched out into television and independent film projects. A combination of syndicated TV comedies, both series and specials, and production of feature films firmly established the Studio Productions team as leaders in creating and producing original programming.

But by 2000, the partners were beginning to feel complacent about their business. The company, while successful, seemed to be standing still. They had reached a moment of truth—change everything or close the doors. In 2001, Studio Productions merged with director Chris Rogers' company, Honest Images, and RuckusFilm was born. It was more than a name change. It was a decision to take their business to a new level. It was their decision to go.

RuckusFilm now develops and produces a wide spectrum of projects, including programming for cable and network television, feature films, music videos, commercials, and corporate communications. Clients include CBS Television, AOL/Time Warner, TurnerSouth Network, and Sony Music.

I sat down with three of the six partners, Clarke Gallivan, Chris Rogers, and Coke Sams to talk about their decision to go. (To see the RuckusFilm brand strategy, visit their Web site at RuckusFilm.com.)

Calloway: Tell me about the rather dramatic metamorphosis of Studio Productions into RuckusFilm.

Gallivan: I think of it as very much a work in progress.

Rogers: We're still having those moments of deciding who we are.

Sams: I think part of being a healthy company is that you can never stop deciding who you are.

Gallivan: You open Pandora's Box.

Sams: And it's a continuing definition of the new thing.

Calloway: There was, though, a specific moment in time when a lot of things shifted. You were doing fine as a company, and yet you decided you needed to go through a significant change. What was that all about?

Sams: It was a decision by a group of people, a coming together by a group of people to make a new thing.

Calloway: Why? Why did you feel the need to make a new thing?

Sams: There was Studio Productions, which was a 20-something-year-old production company that had grown to a certain point and not beyond it. It was just sort of stuck. It had become almost a thing at rest. There was a decision within that company that we wanted to do something new, and we didn't have a clue what it was. But there were at least two of us that said "If we don't do something new within the next year—we're gone." There was a cartoon in the *New Yorker* magazine with two caterpillars inching their way along a blade of grass. One says to the other, "I don't know what we turn into, but it can't come soon enough for me." I think that's the state of mind we were in.

Gallivan: My guiding light at several moments in this business has been that we either shut it down or we move forward, but we do not stay here. But you have to recognize that shutting it down is an option.

Calloway: And about that time you brought Chris in as a partner. Part of the process was new blood.

Sams: Part of the process was definitely new blood. Part of the process is opening yourself up to change and that's where new blood came into the picture. And here was Chris that had change written all over him. You just knew that with Chris, there would be no shortage of a point of view.

Rogers: Just getting to the point where you say, either we kill it or do something different, is a major seismic shift in thinking. Getting to that point is the jumping off point. I had gotten complacent in my business and Studio Productions had gotten complacent in their business. I had built a company that I was proud of and yet I had gotten to a point where I didn't care if I let that go. There was a larger good to be gotten out of changing to something else. You have to get to that point as a company. To the point of recognizing the value of what's come before, but not becoming beholden to it.

Gallivan: The name change to RuckusFilm and the real psychic change came about six months after we joined forces with Chris.

Sams: In my mind it was a very conscious application of the notion of branding.

What if we actually built a new brand? That meant, to me, having a cool name, a cool logo, something meaningful behind it, and people that get it. It all came from the conscious effort to build a brand.

Calloway: To me your process looked like it was truly branding from the inside out. You didn't hire an ad agency and say, "What's a name that will sell?" You picked a name, RuckusFilm, that felt good to you guys.

Sams: Totally. Chris, actually, was the push behind it. This has never been a group that rushes toward concencus. It's purposely made up of contrarians and people with very different perspectives. It's a small company so you don't want a lot of redundancy. Everybody is way different. Chris said, "Commit to this. We sit in a room for three hours and walk out with a new name." We came into this room sat down with dictionaries and thesauruses and picture books and *Bartlett's Quotations.*

Gallivan: And I think it's the only time that all six of us have had that kind of creative coming together and it was amazing. It was amazing.

Rogers: We took 40 minutes.

Gallivan: It was a true brainstorming session.

Sams: Total openness. Nobody shot anybody down. Everybody riffed off of everybody else.

Rogers: And while there were some second thoughts on everybody's part, there remained enough consensus after two weeks that we said let's move forward. And in applying the name we came up with a cool logo that's won awards and something that made us all go "Wow!"

Calloway: The logo is one thing that struck me as significant. You went from being kind of a generically named company, Studio Productions, to being RuckusFilm with this big eyeball as a really wacky logo and everybody here seemed to get a new spring in their step.

Gallivan: That process totally convinced me of the power and importance of visual design.

I think even more than the name, the visual manifestation of the brand, the logo, actually changed everything for me.

Calloway: Is it fair to say, then, that the new name and the new logo was primarily for you much more than it was for the marketplace?

Rogers: Yes.

Gallivan: Absolutely. It is so much easier now to go into the marketplace with the attitude of this new visual presentation. It's more meaningful and more comfortable.

Rogers: It's an attitude we can line up behind. It's an attitude that we can back up. If we come in with a business card that has this crazy, wacky eyeball guy as a logo, it says something about our company when we present ourselves to potential clients. It's like a license to have fun and be creative.

Gallivan: And it also says, "Notice me!" Before it was almost like we were saying, "Don't notice me." I still look at it and just start laughing.

Rogers: The logo design won awards and that gave us a boost. Before long even the doubters among our group were on board wholeheartedly.

Sams: This new sense of ourselves and our edge is what has really brought us together.

We're not referencing an old thing anymore. We're building a new thing and that's something that we're doing entirely together. It's also been way more fun. As we created a new business plan we wanted everything in this new incarnation to be more fun.

Calloway: It's interesting that you approached branding from the standpoint of let's make this more fun for us instead of trying to figure out what would sell best. But ultimately by doing it that way you did get to what would sell best.

Rogers: It was definitely done for us. But it was done with the idea of presenting us to the outside world. And one of the greatest benefits of making this great big decision to make a change is that it's made the whole decision-making process easier for us as a group. By making this huge change, other changes have come easier to us. Things that we used to just talk about we are now acting upon. We used to make decisions to think about things. Now we're making decisions to act.

Keep It Simple and Make It Clear

Larry Morse, president of Quill Corporation, wrote the following article for *Pen Pal,* the company newsletter. In this article, Larry makes the case for staying focused on what's important:

> I am always a little surprised and confused when I hear of companies with books full of mission statements, goals, values, guiding principles, shared visions, shared values, and on and on. What's worse, these books usually wind up collecting dust somewhere. It's easy to fall into that trap. We have all probably done it at some point. I know I have. But the real crime in spite of all the books and good intentions, is that the people in those organizations often don't know what the company stands for or where it wants to go. I once read of a CEO from a major U.S. corporation who actually said that if you asked his top 10 people separately where the corporation was heading; you would probably get 10 different answers. That's not good.
>
> I really believe that the leader of any organization must develop two very important and fundamental truths about that organization: What does it stand for, and where do you want to take it. You can call these things vision, values,

ideologies—whatever, but you must have them. And most importantly, the two truths have to be simple enough for all to understand and embrace, and they have to be made clear to everyone in the organization over and over again until they are embedded as part of the corporate culture.

You can put these truths in books or on little cards or simply talk about them and never put them in writing. But they have to be simple and clear enough to become embedded into the organization. When they are, they will then serve as the glue that holds the organization together in both good times and bad. Whenever there is doubt in an employee's mind as to what to do in a given situation, they should clearly know and understand what the company stands for and where it is going. Knowing these two fundamental things should give them the answer and the direction they need to make a decision or find a solution.

If, for instance, your organization stands for providing quality and affordable health care to citizens in your part of the state, that's pretty clear—lots of things are involved with that—but the focus is still very clear. And if you want to double the number of hospital beds over the next three years, that's a pretty clear direction, too. Everyone in your organization should truly understand that one collective goal and work together to achieve it.

Now, you can sprinkle in some of your values if you like, but your people must know these two key things about the organization—what you stand for and where you're headed. And beyond making these ideals simple and clear, the leaders of the organization have to articulate them, and practice them over and over. You can't come up with the two fundamental truths and then think you have finished the job. You are only just beginning.

There Are No Executives in This Business

Larry Keener is the CEO of Palm Harbor Homes. When it comes to being more than just a manufacturer and seller of a product, I think that Larry "gets it" as well as anyone I've ever known. Larry and his leadership team do a great job of reinforcing on a daily basis the principles that they believe in and operate by.

Calloway: How involved are your company leaders in the day to day fundamentals of the business?

Keener: We have a saying in our company that 'there are no executives in this business.' What this means is that no one in our company can allow themselves to be removed from the fundamentals of building, selling, financing, and servicing creditworthy buyers. Accordingly, we view leadership as principally involvement, commitment, and stewardship.

Calloway: What do you see as being the primary leadership responsibilities?

Keener: Our leadership training and development processes stress leaders as coaches, involved but apart, setting the pace and providing the support our people need to succeed.

Their responsibility is to build teams, produce results, and promotable subordinates. It involves hard choices and sacrifice and requires maturity to understand that the sweetest personal rewards of leadership are in being in service to your subordinates.

Giving Is Receiving

Sometimes a Category of One performer is right under your nose. In this case, her hands were in my mouth. Dr. Cheryl Scott is my dentist. Over the years I have been fascinated with the success of the practice that Cheryl has created with her wonderful staff. She is not only a great dentist, she's an insightful businessperson as well.

Cheryl holds both the Mastership Award, the highest achievement awarded to postgraduate dentists by the Academy of General Dentistry, and the Fellowship Award, which is awarded to postgraduate dentists by the Academy of General Dentistry for continuing dental education. She is a member of the Visiting Faculty for the L.D. Pankey Institute for Advanced Dental Education in Miami, Florida, and she serves on the board of trustees for the Tennessee Academy of General Dentistry.

Calloway: Did you ever have a moment when you felt like you made the decision to make your dental practice something really special? A moment of truth when you truly decided to go to the next level of performance?

Scott: Yes, I had a thrilling moment of understanding 12 years ago, the memory of which is now with me all the time. I had just learned a new procedure. The "scientist/craft person" in me, a common denominator in most dentists, valued this new procedure because it brought a higher level of science and skill to the care I could offer my patients and also a *dramatic* increase in their comfort. Any new skill requires one to slow down, *slow way down* to get it in your head, your hands, and then into your practice.

The life-altering, practice-changing, unexpected joy-fully rewarding surprise for me was not the new procedure at all. What changed my life forever was the way my first patient, John, responded to the level of care.

The presence of time seemed to disappear for me as I treated him. Nothing in the world mattered except bring-ing ALL of myself and my new learned skills to my pa-tient. Nothing mattered except his comfort. That's what John saw and that's what he thanked me for over and over again. Yes, he loved the exceptional comfort of his bite and jaw function as he spoke. He had an immediate apprecia-tion for the fine-tuning and exquisite harmony in his mouth. We finished treatment, he stood up, I was saying my "good-by, see you next time," when unexpectedly he held his hands out, creating a pause in the room, and I knew he wanted to tell me something. As the silence in the room expanded, his eyes looked into mine, he stepped forward and took my hand, and then from someplace deep inside of him came a soft "Thank you" followed by more silence and a handshake.

I cherish that moment often. That "Thank you" meant more to me than I can express. He was thanking me for placing his care and comfort above all else and for staying present, without interruption and without regard for time or money, until that care and comfort was achieved to his satisfaction as well as mine. It was the first time I "got it" that giving *is* receiving. I knew then that nothing in den-tistry could ever be as satisfying for me as that kind of grat-itude. It was at that point that I wanted to change my self and my practice, make it all that I could be, all that it could be. A philosophy of how to practice began to interest me.

I began then to develop a plan for achieving a relationship-based practice.

Later, I deepened my understanding of what happened as I studied the writings of a world famous dentist, Dr. L. D. Pankey. His definition of a "professional" is that quality of conduct which accompanies the use of superior knowledge, skill, and judgment toward the benefit of another person or society prior to any consideration of self-interest. His motto was "quid pro quo," as you give so shall you receive.

Calloway: How important are your relationships with your patients? I'm talking about everything in addition to the actual dental care. One of the things I've always been so impressed with is that everyone that works with you seems to become my friend. It's kind of like going to see my pals when I come there. Is that something that you all talk about and think about?

Scott: Relationship is the single most important thing in life. The trust our patients place in us is sacrosanct. The feeling we have as a team working together to be all that we can be for our patients creates an environment that patients often comment on with statements like, "You have the nicest, most caring staff. I feel like everyone here cares about me and is my friend." As a team, we thrive on this, we are living to the fullest when we get that kind of feedback.

Everyday in the office we busy ourselves with a multitude of tasks and minutia.

We also have regular staff meetings about many topics including: scheduling to stay on time and make a profit, the latest OSHA requirements, operating the practice efficiently, continuing education opportunities to stay current in a rapidly changing field, engaging patients in a manner that helps them want what they need, how to market our practice, et cetera. All these things are important and we enjoy achieving success in them. But what brings us smiles, what we live for are satisfying relationships with our patients, our friends.

The action we take to create and preserve the relationship is to "make time" in our day for relating to people. This means slowing down. "Slowing down" seems impossible to a society that thinks bigger is better, more is better. This action, slowing down, seems anti-productive and unprofitable but it is not. I now know that people who feel completely informed and cared for, people who feel that they are partners with us in pursuit of a common goal (their health, beauty, and longevity), people who are given all the information and time they need to make choices, will ultimately engage in a plan to restore their mouths to total health. An average dental practice treats one tooth at a time. The uncommon practice treats the whole person restoring them to a level of high dental fitness, optimum dental health with the intent of maintaining it for a lifetime.

This is not easily achieved. The pressures of the insurance world of PPOs and HMOs demand that you schedule as many people as possible in a day. A high volume of patients must be seen per day because the PPOs and HMOs who promise their "on the-list" doctors plenty of new patients are setting the fees and those fees have NOTHING to do with real costs. The majority of practices accept PPOs and must run at a high volume all day every day to meet their overhead. I used to participate in PPOs but found they have no place in a relationship-centered practice.

On a daily basis, we discuss what "little things" we might do for patients. Send cards acknowledging events in their personal lives; ask about their family, their lives. We get to know them. We treat them like neighbors and we have fun doing it.

Calloway: You seem to always be going for more education and looking to improve your skills and stay very, very current. Could you talk a little about why you think that's so important?

Scott: Each of us, each person everywhere every day, is always teaching. The thoughts and words we share with others teach our worldview to all we meet. What an important task we all have. We must be good learners to be good teachers.

I feel I am a perpetual student and this brings endless benefit to my staff, my patients, and myself. I have studied so much on a few topics (occlusion, TMJ disorders, and philosophy of practice) and enjoy them so completely that I continue to deepen my understanding of them by teaching. The teacher is the student.

I learn a great deal from patients. Most recently, several of them have revealed an earnest desire that I learn more about the very latest in holistic dentistry. They have learned more on the Internet than dental schools and organizations are teaching. They have asked that I become very current about the health hazards of mercury fillings because they personally want to reduce toxicity. This is important to them and because it is I am beginning to study this field.

Alter the Plan

I wanted the perspective of one of the members of Dr. Scott's incredible staff. I could have picked any of them because the consistency of attitude and performance on her staff is remarkable. I spoke with Victoria Richards.

Calloway: Victoria, what gives your work meaning?

Richards: Making a difference in patient's lives is what gives meaning to my work. Every morning we have a short staff "huddle" to begin the day. We share information about our patients and assess the schedule. From there I form a plan as to the type of treatment each person will need. But that is all it is—a plan—and that plan can be altered.

Calloway: What do you mean by "altering the plan"?

Richards: Altering the plan is where I can have an impact in patient's lives. Like the time one of my favorite patients returned for her six-month appointment and I ask how her husband of 50 years was doing. He had died and I didn't have a clue. I spent the next 20 minutes holding her hand while she cried and reminisced about her husband. Was her dental health the most important thing that day? No. Having me available to listen is really what she needed. At the end of the appointment I walked her out and gave her a hug. She said, "Thank you. I feel better."

Altering the plan has given me the opportunity to make a difference in by encouraging someone to go to their medical doctor to have physical because of changes I see in their mouths. Because I took the time to let them know I care by expressing my concern, patients have had diseases such as diabetes and cancer diagnosed.

People truly do not care how much you know until they know how much you care. Altering the plan is where is how my patients I care. It is where I can have the most impact and make a difference. That is what gives meaning to my work.

It Really Is That Simple

When the right people come together at the right time with a common goal, the improbable can become a reality. Synaxis is bringing the right people together to take advantage of opportunities within the rapidly and constantly changing financial services industry. Synaxis Group, a wholly owned subsidiary of First Tennessee Bank, is one of the largest insurance brokerages in the United States.

In the ancient Greek, Synaxis means, "bring together." David Haynes, chairman and chief executive officer of Synaxis Group, is dedicated to bringing together the people, products, resources, and technology to create a Category of One organization devoted to better serving customers.

Calloway: When selling what some people would consider to be a commodity product—insurance—how do you get beyond price, especially when everyone claims to offer "great service"?

Haynes: You get beyond price by providing great customer service. You anticipate a customer's needs and meet them with all the resources required to provide a solution. It really is that simple. While many companies claim to offer responsive customer service programs or solutions; few actually do it. Clients are very savvy. They understand when they are receiving professional and prompt service and actually get a solution. They value this tremendously.

And an interesting transformation takes place when clients are given a solution and receive great service. The salesperson and his or her company are perceived in a completely different manner. They occupy another position in the customer's mind.

The salesperson is no longer seen as person "peddling" a commodity who must respond to quotas and other restraints placed on them by the company, some of which probably take precedence over client needs. The salesperson who provides a solution and great service is seen as a trusted advisor who puts client needs in front of other requirements that are placed on him or her.

This is an incredibly important distinction that allows a company to leverage its relationships to increase market share. While this may seem like a simple answer, it has been the key for insurance brokers who have continued to increase their business.

Calloway: Synaxis is at a crossroads—moving toward achieving a whole new level of success. When taking an organization to the next level of performance, what do you think are the most important things that a leader can do to make it happen?

Haynes: There seem to be three critical "things" that a leader can do to help move a business to the next level. This is true whether the next level is increasing staff to serve growing client needs, entering into a new geographic market, introducing a new product, or planning for an initial public offering. The first action that a leader must take is to clearly define their vision for the future.

Outlining a vision is more than the short set of sound bites that many of us are now used to hearing from executives on popular cable television business programs, although these are a part of an overall effort to communicate the vision. In order to acquire "buy in" from management, employees, and current and potential clients, a leader must demonstrate an understanding of the challenges that the company will face. This includes advances in technology, pressures from competitors, labor challenges, distribution obstacles, and financing just to name a few.

This adds credibility to the vision and plans that are being presented. Credibility helps to instill a seldom-discussed intangible: believability. Those who must subscribe to the vision must believe the plan presented by a leader is achievable, and that it is not just "another corporate initiative." If people do not believe that a plan is achievable, then the vision will not become reality.

Second, the leader must ensure that management and employees are motivated to achieve the objective. This step encompasses three parts. Management and employees must:

Understand the vision/plan and the benefits that it will bring to the company and to them. Some leaders often forget that the first question people ask when presented with possible change is, "How will this affect me?" That question is often followed closely by, "What's in it for me?" It is a natural progression, and strong leaders understand and prepare to respond to these questions.

Agree to the major tenets offered.

Support the implementation of the vision/plan.

Third, a leader has to be prepared and able to communicate the vision and plans for growth to clients. This communication is focused on responding to the key question that a client has, "How does this change benefit me?"

Clients must be educated about the potential advantages of change in terms that they understand. The most significant mistake a business can make is to try to define shifts in strategy by highlighting the positives for the corporation. Clients typically don't care, unless they are also shareholders. That's why it's important to present advantages during this time. This illustrates to clients that the company has not grown stale and that it is continuing to change and grow *to benefit them*.

Calloway: If you had to pick three keys to success in business, what would they be?

Haynes: First, always begin with the end in mind. In other words, you have to know what you want to do before you can accomplish it. So many times in business, people and organizations fail because they are unable to clearly define what they do and who their customers are.

The second key is people. Always, always hire the best you can find and treat them well.

Third, know thy customer. Understand their needs and wants and provide a solution, not just a product, and actually give great service.

High Expectations from the Start

If I had to pick one individual who exemplifies Category of One performance, it would be Jane Hutson.

Jane began her career as a sales manager for the Berry Company in Yellow Pages sales. In 1987, she joined Cellular One as a sales manager and was promoted to general manager at the age of 27. She was the youngest general manager in the company and one of only four women to hold that position. Jane won the President's Trophy for highest producing market in the company (out of 154) and was also awarded top honors for Customer Satisfaction—Lowest Churn. Jane joined Sprint in 1996 as director of the Middle Tennessee market. She hired her team from scratch, and was consistently in the Top 10 markets in the nation (out of 64) for 4 years.

Jane went to Sprint headquarters in 2000 as senior director of sales and development and sales compensation departments. She developed the eLearning Zone, an award winning training Web site that is estimated to save the company over $15 million over a five-year period. Jane is now back in the field as a senior director, indirect sales and distribution for Sprint, PCS.

Calloway: I have always admired how you keep your teams motivated and focused. How do you do it?

Hutson: My approach is to set high expectations from the start, to hire very, very well, set goals, plan the strategy for achieving those goals, review results on a consistent basis, and hold people accountable through follow up and check points. I believe in celebrating successes and in having fun. One of the best pieces of advice I ever received was from my father who told me to surround myself with brilliant people and I will always enjoy success. I've been lucky and seem to hire well. I don't believe in kicking the ball and dragging people along that are not contributing. It's better to let people pursue other opportunities than to keep them if they are not producing up to expectations.

Calloway: Beyond having a quality product at a competitive price and offering great service, what do you think is the key to creating customer loyalty?

Hutson: I believe customers have to find sufficient value and a sense of "belonging" with the product or company. Loyalty is more than just satisfaction. I believe customers need to know that they will not be let down by your product; or, if they are, that you will make it up to them beyond their expectations. Customers want to be treated as our most important asset in addition to our employees. The most loyal customer feels like they really belong here. That's the objective, the goal—to get our customers to feel this way. The key is to have this as the foundation of the culture in your company. Corporate America tends to focus on Wall Street and not on the customers. If companies would pay more attention to their customers, the "Street" would be taken care of as well.

Calloway: If someone just starting out in business asked you for the three most important ideas you could give them about how to succeed in business AND be happy in life at the same time, what would you tell them?

Hutson: First, listen to your heart and your gut. Always, always, always do the right thing. We are taught at an early the difference between right and wrong. There really is no gray area here. Simply do the right thing. It may be difficult, trying, or even agonizing sometimes, but do it. You will always like who you see in the mirror.

Second, as my father said to me, surround yourself with brilliant people. It will make your life better, more enjoyable, more enriched and more fun. Brilliant people are not necessarily those with the high IQ. Brilliance is found in creativity, humor, productivity, drive, joy of living, loyalty, integrity, grace, and balance.

Last, find out what your gifts are and pursue a life that will utilize those gifts.

Help others to find their gifts and guide them into the areas that will allow them to flourish. It's a beautiful thing to watch someone do what their heart desires and share their special gifts.

Index

A

Achieving growth as a goal,
 55
Advertising, matching reality,
 104–105
Apple computers, 104
Assumptions, dangerous, 8

B

Barrett, Mike, 130–131
Baynham, Frank, 35–36
Benchmarking, 163–165
Berry Company, 213
Blue Cross and Blue Shield of
 Tennessee, 100–101
BMW, 85–86, 116–120
 emotional connection to
  customers, 139
 promotional campaign,
  117–120

Bogus claims, 77–79
Bradley, Bobby, 17, 18,
 44–45, 71–72,
 110–112
Branding, 25–26
Brands, creators of, 104–105
 definition of, 97
 importance of, 97–98
 killer of, 100–109
 telling the story of, 104
Burandt, Mike, 19

C

Calm, creating, 66–67
Cathcart, Jim, 140
Cellular One, 213–214
Change:
 achieving, 22–23
 consequences of not changing,
  59
 dangers of 54–55
 importance of, 51–52

Changing effectively, key to, 65–66

Chaos, managing, 65

Commercials, do not create brands, 105

Commitment to change, 22

Committing to excellence, 6

Commodity trap, 75–96
   avoiding, 81
   transcending, 75–77

Communicating vision, 18

Competitive strength, 65–66

Complacency, boundaries created by, 60–62

Consumer lending company, 5

Core, developing a, 54

Creating processes for change, 21–22

Creative perception, 68

Credit, deserving, 5

Crisis, value of, 3

Crosby, Philip, 4

CST, 17–18, 71–72, 110
   branding, 110–112
   communicating the vision, 18
   culture of, 44–45
   growth threshold, 17
   Launch Card, 110
   mission is you, 109
   relationship strength, 110

Cultures, creating, 48–40
   identifying your, 25

Customer relationship management (CRM), 134–135

Customers, characteristics of, 45–46
   departure signals, 138
   emotional connections with, 139–141
   expectations, 145–146, 158–159

Cycle of success, 63

D

Day-to-day decisions, 41

Deciding to go, 13–14, 16–17

Decisions, making, 3, 39–40
   deliberate, 2
   moment of clarity, 8
   requirements for, 19

Definition, expanding, 4–5

DeGregory, Colleen, 129

DeGregory, Michael, 129

Departure signals, customer, 138

Differentiation, 42, 87–91

Disney, 96, 104, 140, 141

Downturns as validators, 4

E

eLearning Zone, 214

Emotional connections to customers, 139–141

Employees, retaining, 41–43
   sharing a vision, 44

Executive Women International, 143

Expanding our definition, 4–5

Experience, customer, 153

Exxon, 98

F

First Tennessee Bank, 210–213

Fohl, Blake, 183–193

Forward movement, model for, 53–54

Four Seasons Hotel, 47–48

Frankenheimer, John, 118

G

Gallivan, Clarke, 196–200

Georgia Pacific, Consumer Productions Division, 19–20

Gift of Sight Outreach, 35

Gift of Sight program, 34, 38, 46–47

Gluck, Joel, 94–95

Goals, questions about, 14–15

Goal setting, 41

Greatness, creating, 20–21

Greene, Joe, 139–140

Grocery business, 83–84

Growth threshold, 17

H

Harley Davidson, 102–104

Haynes, David, 210–213

H.G. Hill Food Stores, 84

Honest Images, 196

Hutson, Jane, 213–216

I

Improvement as a goal, 54–55

Inarritu, Alejandro Gonzalez, 118

J

Jordan, Michael, 139

K

Kar-Wai, Wong, 118–119

Keener, Larry, 3–5, 203

Kelleher, Herb, 82

King Jr., Martin Luther, 44

Knowing who you are, 24–27, 38–39

L

Land's End, 104

Laura Ashley, 103–104

Leaders, description of, 49
Leadership, definition of, 27
Lee, Ang, 118
Legendary, becoming, 5
LensCrafters, 32–38, 46–47
vision statement, 33–34
Les Schwab Tires, 91–93
Lions Club International, 34
Luxottica Group, S.p.A., 33,
36

M

Management, definition of,
27
Marriott Hotels, 113–114
Mirror, 128–129, 132–133
Mission statement, 29–32
writing, 2
Morse, Larry, 6–7, 16, 23, 71,
109, 120–121, 201–203
Motivation, 27–28
Motivational speeches,
12–13
Movement as a stabilizing
factor, 60

N

New customer reality,
145–167
Numbers, inherent weakness
of, 43

O

Opportunity, creating, 67–68
Outside-the-box thinking,
56–58, 119–120
Owen, Clive, 119

P

Palm Harbor Homes, 3–5,
120–121, 203
People Matter Most campaign,
80
Perception, creative, 68
Powerful language, using,
31–32
Preferred Hotels, 48
Pressure, dealing with, 66–67
Price, dealing with, 81–82
beyond, 82
Produce Marketing Association,
93
Profits, how to make, 25
Promises, false, 77–79
Prosperity, as a danger, 54
Purpose, power of, 28–29

Q

Quality as a differentiator,
84–86, 156–157
Quality Improvement Process
(QIP), 4

Quill, 6–7, 71, 201–203
  brand, essence of, 109
  communication, 23
  decision to go, 16
  leadership model, 16
  strategic imperatives, 7
  thinking outside-the-box, 57
Quill Leadership Institute, 17
Quill Leadership Model, 16–17

R

Reality, new, 63–64, 145–167
  perception as, 67
Requirements for decision
    making, 19
Retaining employees, 41–43
Richards, Victoria, 209–210
Ritchie, Lee, 118
Ritz Carlton, 48, 96, 141
R.J. Young Company, 109
Rogers, Chris, 196–201
RuckusFilm, 196–200
Rules of business, 56, 122–144
  customer rules, 122–125
  knowing more, 123,
    125–127

S

Sams, Coke, 196–200
Scarlett, Joe, 176–177 180–181
  interview with, 173–175

Schmidt Sr., Charles E., 168
Scott, Cheryl, 142, 204–208
Senior leadership teams, 6–7
Service, customer, 154–156,
    159–161
Shaw, George Bernard, 50
Southwest Airlines, 42–43,
    82–83
  competing at the commodity
    level, 83
Sprint, 214
Stability, measuring, 58–59
Staples, Inc., 6–7
Starbucks, 102, 114–116
Strategic imperatives, 7
Strategic plans, 43–45
Studio Productions, 195–201
Success:
  components of, 49–50
    celebrating, 53
  cycle of, 63
  painting a picture of, 16–17
Survival-of-the-fittest, 64–65
Synaxis Group, 210–213

T

Themes for company meeting,
    11–12
Thorobred Motorcars, 150–151
Tire Kingdom, 182
Tractor Supply Company, case
    study of, 168–194
  values, 171–172

Trump International Hotel, 48
Turning points, 2–3, 6, 9

V

Valdez oil spill, 98
Validators, downturns as, 4
Value, 153
Van Hooser, Phil, 40
Vision, communicating, 18
Vision statement, 29–32
Vision vans, 34

W

Weathers, Kelly, 115
Wheaties, 104
Witex, 102–103
Wright, Jim, 181–183

Y

Young President's Organization,
    165

About the Author

Joe Calloway's client list reads like a "Who's Who" in business—from newspapers in Sweden, hotels in Great Britain, and computer companies in South Africa to world brands like BMW and IBM. He is a business consultant and speaker, and has been inducted into the International Speaker's Hall of Fame. Joe owns an award-winning restaurant, Mirror, in Nashville, Tennessee, where he lives with his wife, Annette, and daughter, Jess.